Parrot 1
by Christopher Harris

Text Copyright © 2009 Christopher Harris
All Rights Reserved

Dedication

This book is dedicated to my Mom for kindling my interest in birds and being my partner in crime for so many years as we ran a pet-services business together. We sure have some crazy stories from our time working with birds together in Las Vegas don't we Mom?! Nobody else will ever understand what we went through working non-stop 18 hours per day just so we could get up and work with birds another day. I love you Mom, Thank You for everything – This book is for you.

To Baby Bird, Houdini, Willy and George. To Evelyn Palma, the love of my life. I'm sorry I turned your small apartment into a zoo! To my beloved sons Gabriel and Isaac, I love you! Never give up on your dreams….

Table of Contents

Parrot Training and Behavior 101 by Christopher Harris

Text Copyright © 2009 Christopher Harris All Rights Reserved

Dedication

Table of Contents

Introduction

The Magic 8 Tricks

TRICK #1: Targeting

TRICK #2: Retrieving

TRICK #3: Stationing

TRICK #4: Vocalizing

TRICK #5: Flying

TRICK #6: Memory

TRICK #7: Body Manipulation

TRICK #8: Prop Manipulation

The Importance of Clicker Training and Targeting

Does My Bird Have To Be Trained With food Rewards?

Reinforcement: A Closer Look at Choice & Motivation

Setting up the Sessions – Tips for Successful Training

How Does Your Bird View You?

Is Parrot Training "Flawed"?

Every Interaction is a Training Session

Developing Autonomy – A Note on Trick Training and Parrot Development

Quality Over Quantity

A Note on Clickers

Quick Fix Training Methods

A Note on "Schedule"

Have You "Tried Everything" To Solve A Problem Behavior?

Is My Bird a Boy or Girl?

A Note on Hormones

Say "No" To No

A Quick Tip for Talking

Is it "Cool" To Have A "One Person Bird"?

Understanding the Noise

Taking Skills to a Higher Level

Training Flight with Second Hand or Rescue Birds

Advanced Flight Training

A Closer Look at Diet

Food Management

Weight Management Training Demystified

About The Author

Introduction

My life as an animal trainer has been absolutely amazing. Throughout my time I have met countless birds and have worked with everything from rescues and sanctuaries to pet stores and breeders to Las Vegas magicians and Hollywood movie producers. In this book I am going to share what I have learned along the way. This is a collection of "wisdom", some of it learned hands-on, some of it learned from mentors much wiser than myself, and some learned the hard way. This book is an attempt to give you an inside look at parrot training, whether you want to train tricks, speech, flight, or solve behavioral challenges. These training techniques and tips work. These tricks and tips were put to the test day-in and day-out in the most challenging of situations. In addition to the more "scientific" approach, there are scattered bits tips throughout the book that I think will help you (I have even included a section on nutrition). It is my hope that this book makes a difference in your life and your bird's life no matter what your training goals may be. Parrot Training is, in my opinion, the best way to build a bond between bird and owner. I am blessed to have done what I have and it is my absolute pleasure to share the gift of my experience with you. I wish you and your beautiful birds the very best.

The author pictured with a Blue Throated Macaw owned by the creators of HBO's hit show *True Blood*

The Magic 8 Tricks

I got my first parrot training book when I was still a very young man. My mom worked at an all-bird pet store and I used to volunteer to scrape cages just to be around the birds and learn more about them and this is where I saw the book for the first time. This book amazed me and I thumbed through its pages each time I got the opportunity – it contained at least 100 tricks within its pages and the possibilities for parrot intelligence seemed limitless. So when the store owners' daughter saw me cleaning row after row, cage after cage of bird poop, she jokingly asked me "What bird are you working towards"? When I replied "I just want to be around the birds but if I get credit I don't want birds… I want books!" she laughingly told me to pick any one in the store. Of course I immediately ran straight for the only trick training book and even though it turned out to be the shops most expensive title she let me take it home.

My point here is not to explain the complex tricks that were discussed within this book, because you see, the book taught me a very important lesson as I trained different tricks to different birds as a young adult and soon as a professional avian trainer: It taught me that the different tricks were very similar and could be approached or taught in the same way. And now that I have spent years of my life training birds for casino shows in Las Vegas, working for rescues and sanctuaries, training birds for movie producers and so forth, I learned just how simple the "tricks" could be if I approached them a certain way. I realized that a few "basic" tricks could act as a foundation to build more complex tricks on later.

What if I told you that basically every bird trick in every bird show in the world was only a combination or variation of eight basic tricks and that no matter how complicated a behavior may seem, at its foundation lays one or more of these "simple" yet profound actions? Someone could spend a lifetime creating different ways to do these same tricks and coming up with new variations and ways to do them but no matter how hard someone might try this is basically all there is. You see, as I read the book I didn't realize it but a pattern had begun to play out in my brain and as I taught these same behaviors over and over for a period of years and then shaped them to become "other" tricks it became a clearer picture for me. I have been able to break down the complex behaviors into a more simplified and easier to teach approach.

These 8 "tricks" or behaviors are as follows: Targeting, Retrieving, Stationing, Vocalizing, Flying, Memory, Body Manipulation, and Prop Manipulation.

TRICK #1: Targeting

Targeting is training the bird to touch his beak or other body part to a designated point or "target", such as the palm of your hand, a chop stick, or any other "target" you choose. Giving a kiss is a form of Targeting: the bird simply touches his or her beak to your lips. I often use targeting to teach card tricks, I alter the card imperceptibly and teach the bird to spot the difference. After he learns to select the "correct" card you can mix and match as many cards as you wish and the bird will still choose the right card every time.

This same trick could be used to teach the old gambling game where a ball is placed under one of 3 different cups and they are mixed around to confuse the participant. The bird learns to spot the difference; he touches the target (the imperceptibly altered cup), and picks the right cup every time! Targeting however doesn't only work for tricks, indeed, many "trick" behaviors such as targeting translate well to training abused or neglected birds and also helps to teach basic husbandry behaviors thereby making life easier for the bird and owner. For example, we teach the bird to touch a chopstick with his beak...well, where the beak goes to touch the target the body follows: As the bird attempts to touch the target he could be going inside his cage or a carrier willingly, he could be stepping up onto your hand willingly without really focusing on the fact that he did just step up for the first time (in fact, stepping up onto your hand is Targeting, except instead of touching their beak to a stick they touch their foot to your arm!). The bird could be trained to wear a harness for safety outdoors by luring him with the target so he sticks his head through the straps of the harness. Over time you simply add more snaps and buckles and leave it on for longer periods of time and systematically desensitize the bird to the harness.

Since the bird will move wherever you want in order for him to touch the target, you could teach the bird to run through an obstacle course, come to you on cue (this is called the Recall, an important flight training skill and we will discuss another way to train it later) and so much more. Have you ever seen a couple out on a date holding each other's hands? They were targeting of course! I hope you give this a try, targeting is a great place to start if your bird is fearful or aggressive because you don't need to handle the bird in order to teach it. Try this for fun, teach your bird to target and after they are doing it reliably every time put them on a pair of Roller Skates and show them the target - They will usually be skating circles around the other birds on the block in no time!

TRICK #2: Retrieving

We've all seen someone's pet dog play fetch and our birds are no different. Retrieving is any behavior where the bird picks up and/or transports an object. Usually an object moves from A to B, or A to B to C and so forth but the object is only limited by your imagination and you can make it as complicated as you wish. This is great by itself or you can spice up other behaviors as by adding this to it. We discussed card tricks already where the bird selects a card by Targeting; well you can chain a Retrieving behavior onto that trick so the bird brings the correct card back to the spectator to end the trick.

This is also how the "Dollar Bill Tricks" seen at nearly every bird show and zoo is done – it is simply a flying retrieve! The object that the bird carries and where the object goes doesn't matter: The object could be a scooter that they "ride" (or more accurately carry) back to you. This also goes for Bicycles, Unicycles and so on. Playing Basketball has never been easier, teach them to bring a ball back to a cup or the palm of your hand and then simply cue them to perform this while you hold the cup under the hoop!

I will be using Retrieving for my next project: Teaching a bird to pick pockets for a Las Vegas entertainer. The trick is just a simple retrieve, but I can chain multiple retrieves together so the bird will check the shirt pocket, coat pocket, back pocket etc! Stacking rings on a peg, the "teach and talk bank" and other tricks are all retrieving behaviors and the possibilities are endless. A wedding proposal was even made possible with the help of the retrieve: a simple "Dollar Bill Trick" was made life changing for someone when a Goffins cockatoo returned a different dollar bill to the spectator than the one she had originally had – the bird grabbed the bill from the woman and returned to the trainer and when the trainer told the bird to give her the dollar back this new dollar bill had a diamond ring folded inside of it!

TRICK #3: Stationing

Stationing is useful any time you want the bird to be somewhere at a certain time. It is very similar to the old dog training command "stay" but it is so much more because we can train the bird to be at a certain place at a certain time. When I am beginning flight training with a new bird I am training the bird to Station 99% of the time at first. Where I want the bird to go is different every time, but even though it may look like a completely different behavior, if you look closely you will see it isn't all that complicated. It is very easy to train, most of the time we simply switch from feeding the bird from a food dish to feeding it from a certain place each time. This can be the palm of your hand, platforms that can be placed amongst a crowd, certain points on stage and so forth.

When I train the Recall or when I want the bird to come to me on cue (we discussed another way of training the recall by using Targeting), I am training it to station on my hand, arm or shoulder. I give it the cue (a whistle or upturned palm etc) but depending on the "job" the bird will do I might also train it to station on a perch or stationing platform away from the stage if I need it to "relay" between multiple places. If you are serious about performing with your birds this can make your shows a 3D experience and people will be amazed at the precision with which your birds perform as they fly from one platform to another, then back to you on stage. Many shows such as the LA Zoos "World of Birds Show" have assistants placing tidbits of food in different places throughout the shows, and the birds have been conditioned so that they eat from these platforms every day, so when they are released they fly from point A to point B then back behind the stage or back to the trainer. The assistants often reload the stationing platforms and repeat this several times during the show with many different birds and the crowds are always surprised to have birds coming from all sorts of unexpected places, such as hide-boxes behind them.

This was also done in Las Vegas with the Superstars of Magic Show. Doves were conditioned so that they ate from a specific perch each day and then the perch was placed on stage. When the cue was given during the end of the show the box behind the stage was opened and a gorgeous flock of white doves flew over the crowd so close they could practically touch them before heading to the front of the stage to eat their meal. Stationing can also be used for husbandry and parrot problem solving, such as when a bird picks up the pesky habit of running straight to the shoulder each time: Simply feed his favorite treats only when he sits on your hand and make the hand more rewarding than the shoulder. This way, you've made the bird want to do what you want him to do and he stays where you want him to 100% by choice.

TRICK #4: Vocalizing

A parrot's ability to mimic human speech is one of their most endearing qualities and oftentimes it is what first sparks someone's interest in these intelligent animals and makes them consider parrots as pets for the first time. When somebody is in the room with a smack-talking parrot for the first time they can't help but have fun! The secret to most speech training that I do however lies mainly in capturing behavior. I capture behaviors all the time: Yawning, jumping up and down, nodding the head yes or no – all of these are natural behaviors for many birds and all we have to do as trainers is put it on cue. I do the same with talking. Most people know that to train birds for free-flight and other high-profile stunts I prefer working with younger birds but this is not the case when a talking bird is needed for a TV show etc. For times such as when the History Channel called me and needed a talking bird for a stand-in on a reality TV show I immediately knew it would be a 30-something-year-old Yellow Naped Amazon.

You can teach birds to say things by repeating the same thing over and over but oftentimes parrots learn to imitate the fire alarm and telephone a long time before they start repeating after you, so it is much harder this way. For this reason it is much easier just to capture a word or phrase the bird already says and just put it on cue. For example, those weird sounds your bird learned when you watched Star Trek could be a Laser: If I wanted him to do this noise on cue would wait for him to make the noise, then I would click and say "laser" as I handed him the treat. Soon he will get the idea and you can say things like "What sound is laser" and so on so it is more of a "performance". Or say your bird already knows how to sound like a rooster, you can use a clicker to mark the exact sound you want and then as you hand the bird his treat say "are you a chicken?" You can use whatever cue for whatever sound(s) you want! Audiences love this and you can really get creative.

Most of the talking companion birds learn to mimic is taught in a very passive or informal way and that is fine too, it just might take longer and it involves a lot of repeating the same words, phrases or songs over and over. It can be a bit frustrating at times but it is always worth it and then you can put that on cue as well once the bird has it down. Just be patient – after all, parrots can live a very long time so what's the rush? The best way to train speech in this informal manner is to include the bird in day to day activities and narrate what you are doing the entire time. For example, when the bird has breakfast you can name the foods he is eating, and when you change the bowls you can say things like "yummy" or "water". Say the same thing each day as you carry out the daily routine. Birds will often pick up speaking in context on their own through simple observation and as a way to amuse themselves. This can be a pleasant surprise (unless you cuss like a sailor and your bird seems more and more like a pirate each day!) Don't be surprised when your feathered friend starts answering the telephone or saying "who is it" when a guest comes to the door.

TRICK #5: Flying

Most people and even experienced trainers get a little bit intimidated by flight training but we have already discussed the most important behaviors of flight training earlier with Targeting, Retrieving and Stationing. As I said earlier, a person could spend a lifetime coming up with new variations for each trick and flying is no different. These other flying tricks usually start on the ground. One example is when the bird flies through different hoops. The bird can be lured with the target or a food treat to walk through one or more hoops and then back to you. Over time you simply phase out the lure and work in flight.

Teaching the bird to fly circles can be done easily once you've taught them to fly to you and away from you on cue. Cue the bird to fly to you and in mid-flight just give them the cue to fly away again. You can do this as many times as you like and have the bird flying circles over your audience. Magicians have accomplished this another way for centuries and they still do to this day: They have special noose-harnesses made of a nearly invisible thread that the bird wears and when they toss them into to air the bird has no choice but to fly in a circle right back to the magicians hand. Another way is to clip one primary feather at a time on one wing only. Eventually when they have clipped around 3 or 4 feathers on one wing the bird starts to fly circles. When working with an older bird many people find it is safer to give the bird a "flight-training clip" where the first 3-4 feathers or so are clipped on BOTH wings. This way the bird can still fly back and forth but they are not as maneuverable and they can't really fly up or down or right or left quite as proficiently as before this light feather trim.

Clipping your parrot is an individual choice to make and it is up to you to decide what is best for your bird. Many people think of this "flight-training clip" as a sort of training wheels for parrots and they use this to shape desired behaviors such as the Recall while the birds' choices and ability are temporarily limited. The truth is, much of the ground work can actually be taught to a bird that has been severely clipped and you can just work flight in as the wings re-grow. It might seem odd that you can work on flight training skills with a bird that can't fly at all but a clip is only temporary…what you train can last forever. One game I like to play is to teach a bird to retrieve a small ball etc and really drill it until the bird can practically do it blindfolded and then I start tossing the object in the air and working in more and more flight and height - Audiences love this trick!

Remember that flight training can be very dangerous for your bird so be sure to consult with a professional trainer before attempting it. This requires a very big commitment and is not for everyone so make sure you give this a lot of thought before starting. Some pet owners feel it is morally wrong to clip a parrots wings but it can be deadly to allow them flight without training basic behaviors like the recall – my advice is to view the choice to clip along with your availability to train. It should be with 100% dedication or not at all. If you decide your bird would be safer clipped that is perfectly ok - Remember, there are lots of fun tricks to teach a clipped bird.

TRICK #6: Memory

Most parrot owners will agree that parrots are smart and science is finally coming along to back them up. The truth is, parrots have an excellent memory and we can use this to create some very interesting tricks. Remember the card trick and the old gambling game we discussed earlier? Targeting is not the only way to teach the trick. For many years people simply taught the bird to remember what order the cards would be in. For example, the first time the cards are laid out the correct card is 3rd from the left. Now, to make it appear impossible to cheat the entertainer would lay the cards out furthest on the right the second time (the easiest way is just to place a treat on the correct card so the bird gets the idea. Use the same position each time. Eventually you can start hiding the treat underneath the correct card so he learns to flip it over, then just make the treats smaller and smaller and phase out luring him and instead give him the treat from your hand when he flips the card over expecting a treat. The only limitation using memory is your imagination - Parrots can even learn to play the piano!

The LA Zoo has a raven that "searches" for hidden objects and it is no surprise that he finds them every time because they are always hidden in the same place. The bird just has to remember where the objects are and it's not hard if he's done 2-3 shows a day for 5 years. Psittacines and other birds probably adapted such a good memory because of the intense 3D world they evolved to live in and the same would be true for all birds possessing an "above average" intelligence. It's not surprising to me that they have a large IQ, rainforests are a big place and they had to remember what trees flowered or gave fruit at what time of year and so forth.

TRICK #7: Body Manipulation

The majority of cute behaviors I teach where people think the bird is "almost human" are tricks involving the bird moving, manipulating or in other words animating some body part or in some cases multiple body parts or the entire body. In fact, when I was first coming up with the theory for these "magic 8 tricks" I called these behaviors "Animation Behaviors". These are tricks such as spinning on cue, waving "hi", nodding yes or no, rolling over onto their backs, playing dead, doing flips or summersaults, extending the wings, shaking hands when they meet someone, hanging from the beak on a finger or perch, dancing and on and on. Some of these can be the easiest tricks to teach but some of them can be quite difficult for even the best trainer because many of them involve capturing behaviors the bird naturally does (such as yawning), shaping behaviors by small approximations (have your clicker handy!), physically manipulating the body into foreign positions and so on. These tricks can require a lot of trust between you and your bird sometimes.

Some tricks like waving or turning around can be usually taught in 5 minutes if you have a good relationship with the right bird but some tricks take days before the bird starts to get the idea and even then you might be shaping or fine-tuning the behavior for quite some time. Just start slow and shape the behaviors over very small approximations until you reach your goal. For example, to teach the bird to spin on cue you will only ask it to turn halfway a few times, using a treat or target to lure the bird so he turns halfway as he tries to reach it. After he gets going good and has done a few reps move on so that the bird must now complete a full 360 degree rotation. Then you can start phasing out the lure and moving the cue farther away from the bird with each repetition.

Every bird will be different so move at the pace of your bird and if they just can't seem to move on don't be afraid to go back a step for one or two reps. I can go on and on with instructions for training more Body Manipulation tricks but that could easily fill a book and we have one more set of behaviors left to discuss!

TRICK #8: Prop Manipulation

The final behaviors all involve working with props and like the other tricks there are many variations you can work on to make your tricks that much more complicated and harder to reproduce…if that is your thing. Sometimes it might be easier to start at the end of the trick and work backwards, starting with the finished product first. Opening containers, turning latches, and many other such behaviors are included in this branch of the 8 basic tricks we call Prop Manipulation. Riding a bicycle might be a simple retrieve, but the bird also needs to learn to manipulate the prop with his feet for him to be able to ride it back to you. Many shows begin or end with a parrot unfolding a scroll or banner with "welcome" or "the end" written on it, to do this the bird just needs to untie a knot. Many older props had a lever that was pulled to shoot a bowling ball and knock down all the pins but these are very hard to find these days

One of the biggest secrets to being successful with any prop is conditioning your bird to it so that he enjoys it and doesn't fear the prop or try to avoid it. Many of the birds I supply for shows are raised from infancy to be show birds so I am fortunate enough to begin conditioning them at a young age. If the bird will be riding roller skates and playing basketball I am exposing him to these things before he even has all of his feathers, but don't worry if you don't have this option, you can still systematically desensitize your bird to any object it fears over time. It just might take a while. I suggest you also do this with any costume accessories you plan to wear to your shows, for example, if you will be dressed as a pirate the bird needs to become accustomed to your change in appearance and all the pieces of your costume. This is also a smart thing to do if the bird will work on a television set etc., there are plenty of "scary" things like cameras, wires and cables, flashing lights, pyrotechnics, the audience, cast and crew and so forth. Just be sure that no matter what the bird will be interacting with, whether it is a prop or a piece of costume jewelry, you give them ample time to get used to it.

Conclusion:

Always remember that any and all of these tricks can be mixed and matched to create interesting new show or trick behaviors. I suggest you start looking at a trick and dissecting it or breaking it down into smaller or easier steps. Teach these before chaining them all together to make the "final product". Going to zoos or other animal parks with professional trainers is the best but Youtube.com is a good place to start, one video shows an Alexandrine Parakeet playing golf – how many of the 8 tricks do you see? The bird has to stand in the right spot (stationing), pick up and hold a golf club (prop manipulation), he has to make the golf club connect with the ball (targeting) and then the ball moves from point A to point B (retrieving). Have fun with this and happy training!

The author pictured with two Amazon Parrots in their 30's. These birds are rumored to be aggressive but as you can see they can make wonderful pets. Remember – When it comes to birds don't believe everything they say on the internet!

The Importance of Clicker Training and Targeting

Teaching your bird tricks can be amazing in so many ways, not only can you impress the neighbors with your birds intelligence but the bond between bird and trainer is stronger than that of the average pet owner. There are plenty of other benefits as well; I have noticed that birds who receive regular training sessions aren't as prone to problem behaviors such as screaming and feather plucking and birds that have at least one training session per day are also usually less stressed in new and unfamiliar situations. This process builds confidence in your bird and will help to gain his trust - who could ask for more? If you have recently adopted a second-hand or rescue parrot this would be a great place to start.

DO'S AND DON'TS

Before we jump into training I need to give you all some pointers as to what will make or break a session:

DO: Always end the session on a positive note – this causes the bird to look forward to the next session and makes it a positive experience. If you get frustrated stop the session immediately and just pick up where you left off next time.

DON'T: Train the bird in or on its cage – this is a common mistake many beginners make and it can really complicate things down the line.

DO: Keep the sessions short – at least in the beginning training sessions should be as short as 1-5 minutes.

DON'T: Lure the bird with food – it's ok to show him the treat if he loses interest momentarily but when the bird is chasing the treat around he is more focused on that than the cue you are giving him or the action he is taking. It may seem like he performed correctly but the bird might not be getting the "big picture".

DO: Talk enthusiastically – this makes your bird happy and lets him know what a good parrot he is.

DON'T: Allow the bird to do something it shouldn't – this can damage its confidence when it doesn't know it's doing something wrong but it was given the opportunity. For example, don't get mad at the bird for chewing the couch when you are the one that placed him on it. Set everything up so the bird has the fewest negative experiences possible.

DO: Praise often – your bird will look to you for encouragement as if to say "am I doing ok?" let him know he's a good bird.

DON'T: Punish a bird – the bird has no idea why you are mad and it damages the trust and confidence they have. They do not know it's not acceptable to nip or scream. Always be patient and understanding if the bird isn't acting the way you desire. Try to figure out why it is acting up.

CLICKER TRAINING:
There is a revolution in the past few years that is all the buzz in the training world and that is Clicker Training. It is almost regarded as if it has magical properties by those unfamiliar with it when they first see the results. But what is Clicker Training? The Clicker is a tool for employing positive reinforcement methods that we call a "Bridging Stimulus" or "Bridge" for short. The Bridge doesn't have to be a clicker, it can be a number of things from a whistle to a clap etc, but what the bridge does is let the bird know it did something correctly and food is on the way. This is the golden rule: when the bird hears the click it must get a reward every time. If it gets a click and food doesn't come it starts causing problems. This is why you do not allow your children to play with the clicker and you don't have another "Click Trained" bird within earshot of your current session.

At first you begin conditioning the bird to the clicker simply by clicking and giving the treat for no apparent reason. This teaches the bird that clicks mean treats and this is all they need to know right now. Some birds may be frightened at first but if they are then move slowly and soon they will come to love this. You may even muffle the clicker a bit if the bird is especially scared of the noise. You can let the bird touch the clicker with its beak if you want and this sometimes helps them trust it a little more.

So you just keep clicking and giving the treat but here is another big difference in the way I train from many others: When you give the treat you need to enthusiastically say "Good" every time. Don't say it when you click, only say it when the treat is given. The reason for this is later on in the birds training you can phase the clicker out a little bit. When you go out and see a magician who has trained birds in his show you don't see a clicker in his hand and this is how we do it. Think about it like this: You have a 45 minute show you are about to perform and the bird is clicker trained. Well the bird can be full after just 10 minutes of performing and think about how you feel after a big lunch! So this way you can eventually just reward with praise for the simple tricks and save the big payday of treats for the finale where the bird is required to dive from the top of an 80 foot tall building and land on your arm. If he was full he might not respond as well to the cues and when the bird starts doing his own thing and gets unresponsive then there's trouble.

So click and give the treat and as you hand the treat say "good". It will be quite a while before you phase out the treats but eventually you may need this option and this is your golden ticket. So now you have your bird nice and ready for action. You have trained him how to be trained, what now? Out of the hundreds and thousands of things you can teach the bird what is the most important thing to teach next?

TARGET TRAINING:
If clicker training is your golden ticket to parrot training then Target Training is your magic wand with which to teach literally hundreds of new tricks and behaviors. We discussed it earlier with the magic 8 tricks but here I want to go a little deeper. Are you having a tough time teaching your bird the step up command? I will teach it later by another method in this blog but if that doesn't work Targeting will. How about training a bird to maneuver through an obstacle course? Targeting makes this possible and it is much easier than ever before. What if you want to teach the bird to fly through a ring of fire? Well, we won't get too ahead of ourselves but rest assured targeting is one very effective way to get the job done. Later we will discuss alternate methods to train many of the behaviors you can

teach a bird that knows how to target, but the quickest and easiest way is right here and right now in a much simpler form.

Before you begin you need to first figure out what you will use for a target. Chopsticks, Popsicle Sticks or Wooden Dowels can all make excellent choices, but try to find something small enough that you can hold the target and the clicker in the same hand without too much trouble. Get used to holding the targeting stick and clicker in your "off-hand" which would be the left hand of a right-handed person or right hand of a left-handed person. Holding these in the off-hand allows you the freedom to handle the bird and administer treats with your good hand.

Now that you are familiar with the training tools you can begin. Simply hold the target up to the bird. Usually they reach out and grab it with their beak right away, if so click and reward immediately. If your particular bird seems shy around the target you can start small and reward very small steps until he eventually does touch it. Start by rewarding when the bird does something as simple as looking in the direction of the target. Next you can reward when they take a step toward the target etc., it may take a few sessions until the bird is reaching out to grab the stick, but even the most fearful bird will usually get this in only a matter of days. Don't be afraid to go back a step if needed. Take your time and move at the pace the bird wants to learn. When he gets the idea you can start handing the treats from the other side of the bird's body so he looks like he is running laps back and forth between the target and the treats. Congratulations! Your bird is now target trained!

Where the beak goes the body will follow and the ability to target is so powerful that I highly recommend it as a starting point for training any bird. It is very simple but this is a solid foundation from which you can build on and it is amazing how targeting can be used to train so many other behaviors ranging from basic to extremely complicated. For some birds such as rescue, wild-caught, former breeders or abused parrots handling and stepping up can be considered as advanced instead of beginner training, but if you think about it stepping up is a form of targeting - the only difference is that instead of teaching the bird to touch a target with the beak you are training it to touch your arm with its' foot. Give this a try and your training will be "on target" forever after.

Does My Bird Have To Be Trained With food Rewards?

In my work as an avian trainer I am often asked if every bird needs to be trained using food as rewards. Whether I am consulting with a client for the first time, performing with my own birds as part of an educational show, or teaching a class on avian training this question always seems to come up. The answer of course is no, not necessarily. You actually don't have to train the bird at all. It will still learn of course, whether or not you train your captive "companion parrot" it will still spend its life trying to figure out its' role in the cause-and-effect world it lives in. A parrots' world is a puzzle and they are more than capable of putting mental pieces together with or without our guidance. This is how they survived in inhospitable habitats for millions of years. Left to chance they can develop some very interesting behaviors all by themselves, such as the ability to mimic human speech. This is a double edged sword however, and on the other side of the coin they can also develop some highly undesirable types of behaviors that conflict with sustainably keeping them as pets in our living rooms if we simply leave them to their own devices.

Yes a parrots' world is a puzzle indeed. They are interesting puzzles in their own right though and many people spend a great amount of time trying to piece their particular birds together. Every bird is an individual, with individual likes and dislikes concerning everything from preferred humans to the type of food they enjoy most. Some birds love human attention and affection. Some birds don't. And therein lays the answer to our question. But let's take a closer look.

Most people have heard of Positive Reinforcement but most people still aren't exactly experts on the matter. If you asked most people to define positive reinforcement they would say something like "positive interactions between the human and their bird". But that isn't what PR is. In my day-to-day work what I try to do is increase the frequency of certain behaviors that I want the animal to continue to do or decrease the frequency of undesirable behaviors that I or my clients don't want them to do. To do this I find something that the animal sees as valuable and use it to create receptivity and motivation to do the things I want them to do and to behave the way I want them to behave as closely as possible within reason. By opening or closing the window of opportunity to earn these desirable rewards (called reinforcers) I can communicate with the bird and make it advantageous to the animal to do behaviors more often or less often and get them to choose to do these behaviors that I want them to do. The animal becomes a willing participant and partner that carries out my requests willingly and interacts with me completely voluntarily and by choice.

For centuries mankind relied on tactics such as dominance, violence, fear, and so on to elicit change in another creature's behavior (human and animal) but Positive Reinforcement is training without force or coercion. An animal will work to the least amount required to either earn a positive stimulus (or "positive reinforcer") they see as valuable or work to the least amount required to escape or avoid a negative stimulus (or "negative reinforcer"). So anyone attempting to train an animal has a choice: Do you make the animal work to earn something or avoid something? Many people are actually uncertain as to which method they are employing as they set out to train their companion animal. Luckily for us there is a fool-proof method you can use to distinguish between the two if you have any doubts. All you have to do is ask yourself the question "does this animal want to do this - or am I forcing it to do this"? If it is forced to do something it is Negative Reinforcement.

Now that you have been armed with this information you can probably tell the difference between Negative Reinforcement and Positive Reinforcement but many trainers still do not know that there are different types of Positive Reinforcers you can use as rewards to sufficiently motivate your bird and create a healthy level of receptivity. These two kinds of reinforcers are: Primary Positive Reinforcers and Secondary Positive Reinforcers. Primary Reinforcers are things the animal needs to survive. Because of this they are bio-mechanically hardwired to see them as valuable when we use them as rewards during training. Food is a Primary Reinforcer and the most common of all reinforcers for animal training. They need it to survive and there is no such thing as a non-food-motivated animal so it works for any animal. Water, air, and sex are also Primary Reinforcers that have been used to my knowledge and again they are all Primary Reinforcers because they are necessary for the animals continued existence. Any stimulus the animal needs in order to survive is a Primary Reinforcer.

Secondary Reinforcers are not necessary for an animals' survival. They are stimuli that the animal learned has value so they work to earn it. The problem is, unlike Primary Reinforcers not every bird will work for them because, as we discussed earlier, different birds will assign a different value to any given stimulus. They don't need them to survive so it is simply a matter of how valuable the item is to each individual animal we are working with. This is why I cringe every time I receive a call from someone asking me to train a companion parrot that came from a "bad home" but they want the bird to "work for love, not food". The problem is, while many birds do see human attention and affection as valuable, and will enthusiastically try to earn these Secondary Reinforcers, many birds do not see human attention or affection as valuable at all – especially the birds coming from formerly abusive homes. Imagine trying to train a hawk using cuddles as a reward! So since these birds see me as something to fear and avoid at first I must pair myself with a valuable stimulus, and since all animals are motivated to find and consume food, a favorite treat is usually what I will use instead of wasting my time with the Secondary Reinforcers.

The problem herein however, is that in my experience many trainers will see the Secondary Reinforcers as inferior reinforcers and therefore they will rarely, if ever, use them in the course of their work. I couldn't disagree more and it is my opinion that the highest forms of training lay within these Secondary Reinforcers. Sure not every bird will work for them the way that every bird will work for food but if you can take the time to understand the individual bird you are working with and gain a little perspective into the unique likes and dislikes of that individual it is my experience that your working relationship will only improve. So many trainers are employing weight management. Weight reduction is their solution for an undesirable show bird, when the answer could be as simple as a play or social interest that the bird has. Say for example, that you want the bird to fly laps back and forth from point A to point B but the bird only does 5 reps of the recall before he starts to get full and unresponsive. If a trainer wants more laps from the bird they would typically lower the birds' weight to create more drive or motivation to work. The birds desire to earn food rewards increases so the trainers' behavior is reinforced and the frequency of his behavior increases. But what if the bird has a really good relationship with one particular handler and flies to her any chance he gets? Couldn't that be used to your advantage? Let me rephrase that: shouldn't you be using that naturally occurring motivation to your advantage?

Negative Reinforcement was the go-to or default method humans used to train animals for centuries and so it is still around today, taught by parents and schools as they discipline the next generation of animal trainers, teachers and parents and while this trend is declining slightly it may be around for quite some time to come. Increased weight reduction also works much of the time when behavior change is desired so it too shall continue. But just because it gets results doesn't mean there isn't a more positive solution. I am not saying to abandon weight management altogether, but as time goes on we will see there are multiple ways to achieve the same goal and as trainers in this day and age we have an ethical responsibility to seek the most positive solution available to us.

I believe that by utilizing the different reinforcers there will always be multiple choices available to a trainer when the goal is sufficiently motivating an animal and getting it to do something you want it to do. In my training classes I often use the example of a parent that wants his or her child to clean their bedroom. We could offer the child his favorite food in exchange for completing the task you assigned. The stimulus the child would be working to earn is Pizza, his favorite food and a Primary Positive Reinforcer. The next option involves Secondary Reinforcers. Since each child would view different stimuli with varying degrees of value you might have to see which one he responds to the best. You could say, "clean your room and you can have $5", he doesn't need money to survive but he has probably learned that money has value so he will work to the least amount required to earn it. You could also offer to let one of his friends sleep over in exchange for completing the task, or get him a new game or new toy. You are only limited by your imagination. With sufficient attempts and observation you will usually find something that works to motivate each individual. I have a cockatiel that goes crazy for paper bags and water bottles – who knew that would be so valuable to him? The third and final option would be to present an aversive stimulus that the child works to escape or avoid. This typically sounds something like "clean your room or your dad will spank you". Of course this can work and in all probability it will work but there are repercussions to training with Negative Reinforcement such as aggression, apathy, fear-based responses, and so on. And we just listed several other possibilities that are more positive solutions.

It is at about this time many people begin to see the light but they still don't understand how best to use certain reinforcers or when to use them. For example, what if my bird works great when I use sunflower seeds as a reward but he also really likes peanuts and sees a certain toy as very valuable? Typically what most trainers do in this situation is called Differential Reinforcement. By substituting different reinforcers during the course of a training session you can sometimes keep the bird interested for longer periods of time (for example, if the bird is getting food rewards only 50%-75% of the repetitions because they are getting non-food rewards the other 25%-50% of the time they don't get full as fast and therefore remain receptive to food rewards for longer periods of time). Many trainers also believe that it is mentally enriching, more stimulating and not as "boring" for the bird to receive multiple forms of reinforcers throughout each session.

In my time as a student of Sciences of Psychology and ABA I have learned about something called "Maslow's Hierarchy of Needs" during an examination of motivation and I found it very interesting when applied to positive animal training strategies. For humans the Hierarchy of Needs says that certain needs are more important than others and that the needs of each level must be satisfied before moving on to the next "level" or set of needs. I believe that this is applicable to our birds, at least to some extent and that it is possible to take a subject working for a variety of reinforcers and use the Hierarchy of Needs as a strategy for how, when and why to reward the bird with different reinforcers. The first "level" is Physiological Needs. The rewards you give at this "level" would be Primary Reinforcers. We begin training the bird with food rewards until he starts to get full and ideally right before he starts getting unresponsive. The next "levels" include Safety Needs and Belongingness and Love Needs. Earlier we discussed using the bird's natural preference for a certain handler to our advantage. This level of the Hierarchy of Needs is where this and other Secondary Reinforcers would be used by the trainer. The bird isn't as motivated to earn food rewards but perching on the tallest point they can find is very rewarding and valuable to many birds, so perhaps you could have an adjustable stationing platform raised so the bird can fly up to the top, then after a moment the favorite handler appears and calls the bird down for some of the head scratches he enjoys so much. Many psittacines bond very strongly to their mates and that can also be used. For a bird that is very bonded to his mate, they will almost always go wherever the mate is. My point is we can have a bird that is still responsive and "performing" even though his motivation for food is low. All we have to do is put the puzzle together and figure out the individual animal.

In closing, I cannot stress enough how important food management and "training diets" are to our pet birds. Creating motivation and receptivity is vitally important to keeping parrots as companion animals in captivity sustainably. Training should be about getting the animal to make the right choices even if there are other options available to him. By creating proper motivation we make the animals *want* to do what we want them to do. We create willing participants. We also provide incentives for the animal to do things he or she otherwise might not choose to do, such as interacting with strangers, wearing a harness, entering or exiting a cage or travel carrier, allowing a vet to groom him, and so on, and cause the animal to *choose* to do these things. We can't force a flighted parrot down from the top of an 80-foot-tall auditorium but we can be the better option that the light-fixture. We can make it to the birds advantage to behave a certain way and food management is one way for the "average Joe" and professional trainer alike to get this done in a positive, non-intrusive fashion.

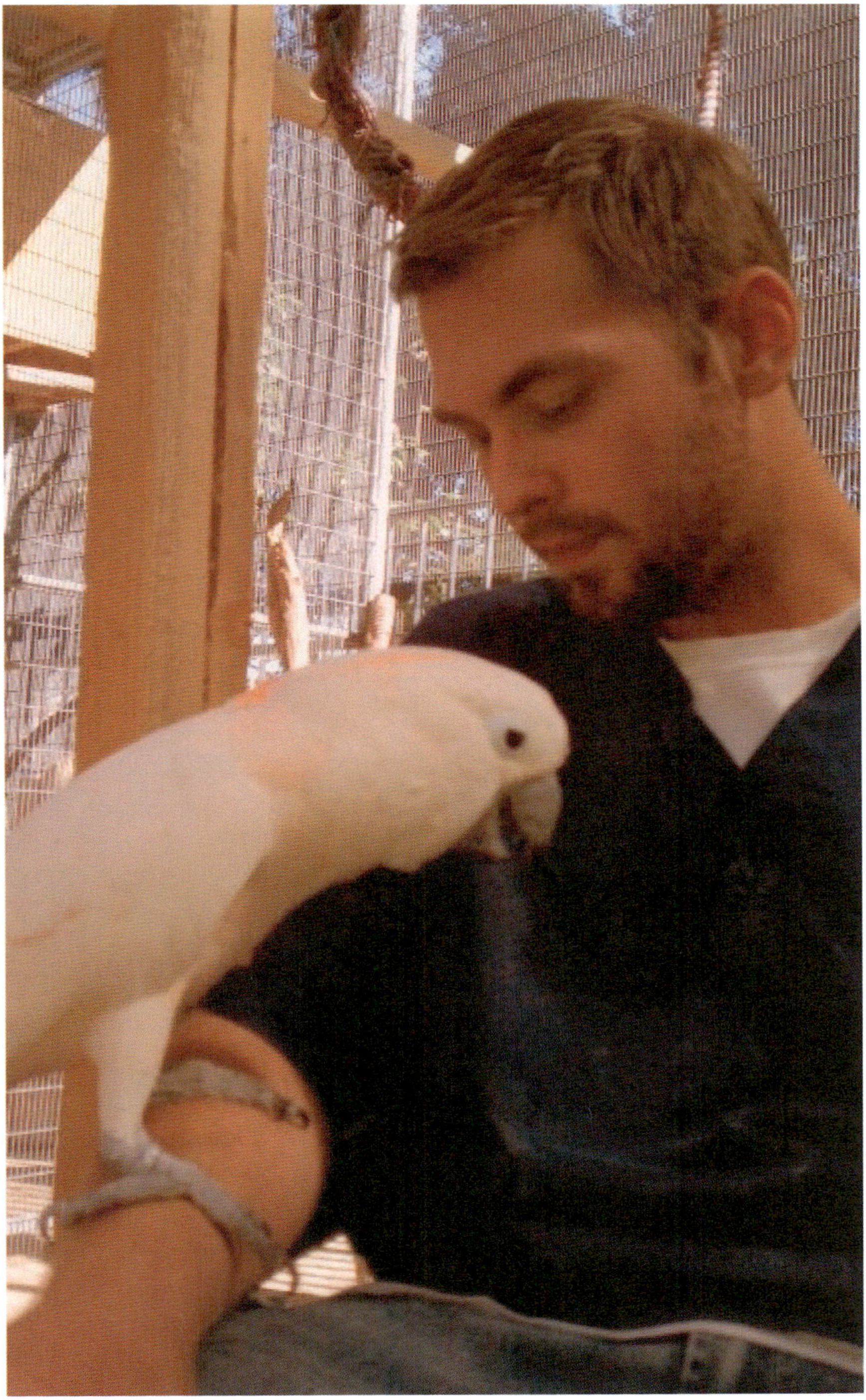

The author pictured with a Molluccan Cockatoo, one of the biggest (and loudest) cockatoo species. There are entire websites devoted to keeping people from purchasing these birds due to supposed aggression but these can be very gentle giants if you raise them right!

Reinforcement: A Closer Look at Choice & Motivation

Animal training is a form of communication. Through hard work we can bridge the gap between the human and animal mind but much of our success relies on properly motivating the bird to want to do what we want them to do. If we are seeking the most positive and least intrusive solution to achieving a goal in modifying or creating behaviors, eventually we must accept the importance of choice and realize the only way to achieve long-lasting results is to understand why our birds are motivated to do the things that they do. Why do our birds fly to us from the top of a 400 foot tall building? I can guarantee that if given a choice, they wouldn't respond well to us if we relied heavily on forcing them to do things. Therefore we must find a way to allow them choice, but also influence their decisions at the same time so that they are choosing what we want them to choose more often than not.

We can't make them fly back to us with threats of punishment but unfortunately this is the way we humans are taught to approach everything from education to animal training to disciplining our children: threats, punishment, and the use of aversive stimuli that the animal tries to escape or avoid. This is our default or "go to" tool for which to illicit change in behaviors. We make the subject avoid a negative stimulus. Many people are aware of the terms Positive Reinforcement and Negative Reinforcement but even some very experienced animal trainers I have known only see the tip of the iceberg when asked to define them, so how can we expect the average companion parrot owner to grasp the concepts besides in very general terms? It is my goal in the following few pages to lay out in fairly simple terms not only the differences and descriptions in our choices of different reinforcers but also to explain how we have multiple options to choose from in every situation. In order to find the most positive and least intrusive solution we must learn to see that there are multiple solutions to choose from.

Why do humans and animals do the things we do? Is it because we enjoy it? Because we have to? What other options are there? What is in it for us? What is behind the behavior? Scientists such as John B. Watson and B.F.Skinner started asking these questions nearly 100 years ago, and we are still learning more every day. Now many years later we understand not only how and why animals can be motivated to behave the way we want them to but we have a language that transcends the barriers between human and animal minds. This language is what we use to train the animals to perform any given trick or behavior that we see in shows and on the big screen. The animals are conditioned to behave the way they do, and this is where the term Operant Conditioning, which is the term used to describe the way we train animals (and even humans), gets its' name.

Behavior is fascinating! Anybody who has ever marveled at the intelligence of a performing parrot or sat in awe as they witnessed a free-flight demonstration involving trained birds of prey can tell you how wonderful it is to see the science of behavior at work. There are examples where experiencing animal behavior at work can be not as enjoyable however, such as when the family dog continues to destroy the yard every night by digging potholes or emptying the contents of your trash cans all over the yard.

The secret to understanding just what it is that causes the animal you share your life with to act the way it does it to find the motivation behind each action. What happens after the animal does something? The trained Cockatoo who just told the audience "Hello" gets a food reward after he performs the behavior correctly on cue. The dog that destroys the yard every night might get screamed at time and time again but it just can't help itself when there are so many delicious treats inside the can.

When we look at the reasons behind a behavior we can understand the animal from a different perspective than we have previously had in the past. The bird who bites isn't trying to be mean, because revenge or grudges are human experiences. No matter how convincing it might seem, animals do have emotions, but they are not the same as human emotions. Is the animal a breeding age Macaw defending its' perceived nest or territory? Was he startled because you moved too quickly? Has he learned that biting gets him the type of response he desires in that particular situation? All too often we arrive at an anthropomorphic conclusion with no basis on facts, but science is entirely based on facts and data that can be checked and rechecked. Operant Conditioning and Applied Behavior Analysis are sciences; unfortunately not every pet owner has a PhD.

To understand how it is we train and motivate birds or any other living organism regardless of species we need to understand what Operant Conditioning is exactly. Merriam-Webster's' Online Dictionary defines Operant Conditioning as: conditioning in which the desired behavior or increasingly closer approximations to it are followed by a rewarding or reinforcing stimulus. The goal of OPC is to make a behavior or reaction second nature. The definition of Second Nature in the dictionary is an acquired habit or tendency in one's character that is so deeply ingrained as to appear automatic. So in essence, when we are training using Operant Conditioning we are conditioning a living organism to perform a behavior(or at least come closer over many approximations) using a reward (stimulus) of some kind until the behavior is so deeply ingrained that it appears natural or automatic. A "Reinforcing Stimulus" can be either Negative or Positive in nature, and there are Primary Reinforcers and Secondary Reinforcers that can be used.

Positive Reinforcement is the foundation upon which all progress with an animal is built upon. Animals can be trained using both negative reinforcement and positive reinforcement, however negative reinforcement relies on the use of aversive stimuli which is something an organism views as undesirable or unpleasant and the animal will only work to the level required to avoid the unpleasant situation. This is why Negative Reinforcement is sometimes referred to as "Escape/Avoidance Training". The animal can be trained with these aversive stimuli, but oftentimes side effects such as fear responses, apathy, aggression or many other behaviors can appear. Giving a response to a negative behavior only reinforces it, the perfect example is when a bird screams incessantly so you give it a treat or yell at it in an effort to make the behavior stop. It might seem obvious that giving a treat to a screaming bird will only result in more screaming but many people do this all the time because the neighbors have complained or you have simply had enough for example.

Any response can be viewed as reinforcement, whether it is simply giving a trained bird a reward for a job well done, or to use my earlier example of reacting to the screaming bird by running up to it and telling it "No", the bird has still gotten a reaction even if it was bad attention from a humans perspective. A bird can certainly learn that screaming or biting can get a response that it desires and in my opinion that is when a behavior becomes problematic, because then the bird is the one running the show, if the bird is running the show then the bird is the one training you. The reason I say it is a problem is not because of the birds perspective at all, the reason it is a problem is because this is about the time in a parrots life that the owner will typically begin to seek an escape, whether it is to abuse or mistreat the animal, hire a Behavioral Consultant or Trainer, or to simply relinquish the bird.

The correct implementation of Positive Reinforcement is simply to reward a behavior the trainer desires, while all behaviors you view as undesirable (screaming in parrots for instance) are ignored and receive no response. An animal can quickly learn that acting in a particular way will yield a particular result, which the parrot views as favorable or desirable. If this were written as an equation it would be A+B=C. A (behavior) +B (reaction) =C (Result). The behavior (A) can be good or bad as viewed by the trainer. It could be talking, Biting, Screaming, a Trick and so forth. The reaction (B) can be a reinforcer such as a treat, it could be a rewarding action such as giving the bird a head scratch or it could be a punishment such as yelling at it because it did something wrong. The result (C) is the behavior changing in frequency, happening either more often or less often because of the reaction to the behavior.

This equation for using positive reinforcement can be used for any behavior, whether you want the frequency which it is displayed to increase or decrease. Let's say the bird says something you enjoy (A) so you give it a favorite treat as a reward (B), and afterwards the bird tries saying the word or phrase again because he enjoyed the reward and wants another one (C). You have just caused the bird to behave in a certain way because it enjoyed the outcome and will work at the level required to earn another food reward. Now let's look at the same equation used to respond to a behavior that you don't want to continue. The bird screams (A), so you leave the room (B), and since the bird equates screaming with you leaving it learns not to do it as often because his favorite person goes away when he behaves that way (C). It may take some time for the process to sink in, but eventually the bird will put 2 and 2 together and realize his or her actions are affecting the outcome of his situation either favorably or unfavorably. This process is the basis behind every attempt to train animals (whether it is successful or not and whether the trainer realizes it or not) and is even the underlying cause that humans to behave the way we do as well. This equation is equally at work in our day to day relationships and every decision we make. The question is: What's in it for us?

The reaction (B) is where the reinforcement occurs and is the most important part of the behavior equation.

Setting up the Sessions – Tips for Successful Training

The best training sessions are set up the day before. To maximize results try to stay one step ahead and set your bird up for success. You can do this in several different ways, a few good habits to get into are:

MAKING A TRAINING PLAN (This is a road map of directions from A-Z detailing how you will accomplish your goal step by step over many small approximations - Don't be afraid to make changes though! Sometimes things don't go according to plan).

PROPERLY MANAGING DIET (This is the big one. Most people give their birds one big bowl of food per day and that is it - don't do that! For most people the biggest problems are helped by sticking to a healthy training diet where food is given twice a day for about a half an hour or so before being removed and then making absolutely sure that your birds favorite foods are reserved for training - no cheating! This is crucial to having a bird that is properly motivated when he is supposed to be and ensures he will be receptive to you come training time. I have worked with many birds that had been abused or mistreated and were terrified of humans and this was the key to my success. The way it works is if he is used to getting his first feeding at 8am for example, he will be more motivated and receptive to training if you work with him right before that feeding time than if you were work with him right after. Just schedule your training sessions about a half hour before each scheduled feeding and that is enough for many people to start seeing results with birds that were previously unresponsive to them or even outright aggressive. It has helped me with managing many different behavioral problems as well as training birds to do a wide range of show behaviors. How well you do here has a huge impact on how well your session goes tomorrow. Remember though - He can eat as much as he wants during training sessions - we do NOT withhold food, we manage it. If you still aren't convinced to start doing this with your bird, consider that it is both mentally and physically healthy too. Studies are showing again and again that it is MUCH healthier for a captive animal if he gets the bulk of his food from training and foraging than a boring bowl of food sitting in the enclosure).

PLAN TO LIMIT DISTRACTIONS (Turn off the phone at the scheduled time or limit any other distraction and really give yourself the gift of being present with your bird. It is important to set yourself up to be as successful as possible and this is one thing that really helps).

MAKE AN APPOINTMENT (Make a strict appointment and set aside that time for your bird and stick to it the next day. It doesn't have to be the same time everyday but when you do decide on a time treat it with the same dedication you give your job. And if you need to do 2 sessions - do 2 sessions! You'd be amazed what you can do with 5-10 minutes 2-3 times per day!!!).

KEEP A JOURNAL (This is the opposite of the training plan - it's a guide to what you just did instead of a guide to where you want to go. Keep track of successes, failures, record the birds weight, record what behaviors you covered that day and how many repetitions they did etc., soon you will be surprised to see how far you both have come together! Keeping a journal helps you to see what is working and what isn't and lets you be a step ahead for tomorrow's session).

LOOK FORWARD TO THE SESSIONS (Get excited! Every day you are getting closer and closer to your goal - even if it doesn't feel that way sometimes. Whether you are training "tricks" or husbandry behaviors, or even retraining/rehabilitating a problem parrot etc., each day you are coming one step closer to that new relationship. Many people seem to be racing towards some imaginary finish line with their birds - but it shouldn't be that way. Realize that this is YOUR TIME TOGETHER and that the training should never end. Keep it fun and enjoyable for both of you. There is no stronger bond with a captive animal than that between the trainer and animal. Don't be in such a hurry that you miss that).

How Does Your Bird View You?

If we examine the definition of stress in humans, the clinical description would be that stress is an emotional and physical response to stimuli. So since it is a response to stimuli it is caused by stimuli and the way those stimuli are perceived. A typical child isn't afraid of cotton balls or Santa's beard but a child can be conditioned to fear these things from a young age (see "Watson's Little Albert Experiment"). The same goes for parrots in the home or on stage. One individual may interact just fine with new people and even enjoy it, while another may be terrified at the first sight of someone new walking into the room. Each bird is an individual and can be expected to respond differently to the same stimuli. Each bird will view things as neutral, positive, or negative individually. The question is how does your bird view you?

If stress is a physical response, you will see that it is actually a biological reaction. This reaction can take many forms as the animal attempts to cope with a negative stimulus: Fight or flight - Heart rate will be increased and so will respiration. Muscles will tense. Activity will also increase in the Parasympathetic Nervous System. Adrenaline glands will begin to secrete Epinephrine (Adrenaline) and Norepinephrine.

But how does a bird come to see things as good or bad? Why does it happen? For the answers to these questions we must turn to the old Psychology Class 101 "Theory of the Mind". Think about it like this: When a bird is born everything is neutral. As time goes on it learns that warmth, food, parents and so on are good, and things like being cold, hungry, or startled are bad. Over time the bird starts forming opinions about the world it lives in - but originally the entire world was neutral. A psychologist named John B Watson worked with this idea many years ago with The Little Albert Experiment where he conditioned a young child to fear cotton balls, beards, mice etc., basically anything that was white and fuzzy. All he had to do was pair these objects with an aversive stimulus. He discovered that any stimulus can be neutral, good, or bad in the eyes of a subject but not only that, he learned that we can change how the subject viewed a particular stimulus. It really is just a matter of perception. It is a very interesting experiment that would have been illegal today (since it was experimentation on humans) , but we aren't so different from our birds in this way and it applies to them as well as to us humans.

My clients often tell me at the beginning of our time together that they want their bird to work for them out of love, not just for food. Unfortunately for them a rescue bird that has been abused in the previous home usually doesn't see human attention as valuable; therefore they will not work to earn that secondary reinforcer. That does not mean this bird would be untreatable, we just have to find suitable reinforcement that the bird does see as valuable, such as sunflower seeds (a primary reinforcer), so that we can offer the bird sufficient payment for a job well done. By digging deep into our trainers' toolbox we can find non-invasive solutions for behavior modification that does not rely on weight management, which is the most common way to elicit responses favorable to the handler in modern day animal training. It does work but there are always multiple options and we should always seek the most positive solution. Animals working at higher weights are healthier, less prone to succumb to infectious diseases, and so on.

Many times when I am working with an animal for the first time it is suspicious, fearful. It sees me as something to avoid. To change this view and make myself more "valuable" I pair myself with a stimulus that the animal sees as valuable. A favorite food works very well. I have found that by taking the favorite food item and ensuring that the animal gets it from me every time I interact with him I can change his perception of me from something to fear and avoid and transform myself into something he or she willingly interacts with. In fact, with consistency I become something that the animal anticipates or even actively looks forward to working with. At first the bird may not even take a food item from my hand even though I know he is fairly hungry. As time passes however they begin to come closer and closer as the scales tip in my favor and begin a new relationship with that bird. This happens simply because of identification and association.

This approach can be applied to all manner of different things that your birds will encounter or work with or around that they could possibly see as aversive (or in other words "bad" from their point of view). A pirate costume may appear very frightening to your particular bird. The best course of action would be to systematically desensitize the animal to your sudden change in appearance by making it a positive thing little by little. Many birds are afraid of hands. But what if every time your bird had ever seen a hand it received a bounty of preferred food items? Would it have the same reaction? Of course it would view hands very differently. The same goes for less preferable people in a birds' life. I had a trainer whom I respect very much ask me what I do in the case of a "one person bird". He seemed to think it was a hopeless case for the thousands of homes in the world where parrot owners have experienced this problem. While it may be true that many species of psittacines are monogamous in the wild and so they often bond to one owner and shun the attention and affection of other members of the household now that they live here in captivity, that does not mean we cannot foster a sort of business relationship with the less-favorite human so that the bird will at least interact politely. By strategically pairing the person with stimuli the parrot views as valuable, and managing this "resource" effectively, the person can also become valuable in that birds eyes. Again, how does your bird view you?

The author flight training a Blue Throated Macaw

Is Parrot Training "Flawed"?

Man has been training birds for over 4000 years. Ever since the first falconers strapped a raptor to their glove and began training hawks and falcons for hunting and pest control a relationship was formed that still lasts to this day. Avian training as with all animal training has come a long way since then. For 100 years animal training has been a legitimate scientific venture thanks to the work of people like Dr. Pavlov, John B. Watson and B.F. Skinner. Today we train animals in a world of variables, statistics and verifiable data that can be checked and rechecked.

Times change however and with it so does accepted facts and practices. The world's finest scientists once believed that the earth was flat. We also used to believe that the Earth was the center of the universe and it was heresy or a crime against the church to suggest otherwise (and those that did dare to wonder committed a crime punishable by death). We must always give thanks to these forefathers of science for without them we might still live in a world clouded by myths and superstition, where science was a crime. The best way to give thanks in my opinion is to continue on in our quest to unravel the secrets of the universe and to think outside of what is accepted and what is not and boldly step out into the fringes where new ideas and hypothesis are waiting to be dreamed. It is with this in mind that I ask the simple question: Is a 100 year old system of animal training truly the end of the road for us – or is our world still "flat" when it comes to avian training?

Scientists have known since the 1960's that Operant Conditioning was flawed. Two brilliant scientists, a husband and wife team named Keller and Marion Breland, published a study called The Misbehavior of Organisms in 1961 and within the pages of this report lies information so important for trainers to understand that it is baffling to think that so many professionals have never heard of it. The Brelands studied directly under the infamous Dr Skinner, whom we can thank for our present-day training methodology and even "modern" training tools such as the Clicker. What they came to realize after working with a wide array of animals was that eventually the trained behaviors and conditioned responses began to break down over time in many cases. The animals' behavior began deviating from the established routines and the conditioned responses. The question the Brelands wanted to know was why this happened and their paper The Misbehavior of Organisms is where they published what they had learned.

As they trained thousands of animals over many years a particular pattern began to emerge that they called *Instinctive Drift*. Simply put, naturally occurring behaviors were invading the training sessions and the behaviors their animals were trained to perform. In their own words they were "fighting a running battle" with instinct. Over and over again they give detailed accounts of how they could successfully train an animal to do any number of behaviors on cue yet many times there was a breakdown of conditioned operant behavior.

One example the Brelands used to describe instinctive drift involved common Bantam Chickens. The Brelands attempted to train a chicken to stand on a platform for 10-15 seconds and after doing so the bird would earn his reward. This did not work out quite as planned however because over 50% of the birds developed a habit of scratching at the platform with their feet instead of just sitting there calmly and this "misbehavior" became more persistent as the length of time the bird was required to stand was increased. To make matters worse for the trainers, about another 25% of the chickens developed other behaviors such as pecking at the platform or at other spots on the ground outside of the platform. That means over 75% of the birds they attempted to train this to were deviating from the established, conditioned behaviors! This happened even though the majority of their birds had performed correctly several times in most cases and often knew what was required in order for him/her to earn the reinforcement.

It is important to note that these behaviors came as a shock to the Brelands because there was nothing in the science of Behaviorism that prepared them for this problem. Early behaviorists threw ideas like instinct out the window and even today many modern trainers are not equipped with the knowledge of what is causing the "misbehavior" and how they can work around it. Some of the animals had been working for years before this phenomenon spontaneously appeared and invaded their trained behaviors and it took some time before instinctive drift was understood. After writing nearly two pages of detailed accounts of misbehavior the Brelands go on to say, "The examples listed we feel represent a clear and utter failure of conditioning theory". So even though many techniques developed almost 100 years ago are still in use today, the Brelands clearly believed that animal training theory as they knew it was flawed – and they knew this back in 1961!

Luckily the husband and wife team began to unravel the mystery of this phenomenon and after a time they came to realize that "These particular behaviors to which the animals drift are clear-cut examples of instinctive behaviors having to do with the natural food getting behaviors of the particular species". The chickens that were scratching the platform and pecking around instead of simply sitting calmly on the platform were reenacting a natural foraging behavior of scratching at dirt and pecking at the ground which they would naturally be doing in order to feed themselves.

So what does this mean for the modern day avian trainer? Consider for a moment that for the last century trainers have essentially treated all animals as interchangeable, using "one-size-fits-all" approaches to train them. We approached tigers the same as dolphins, parrots are trained the same as dogs and so forth. Even though positive reinforcement, applied behavioral analysis, and operant conditioning *do* work, the truth is a Cockatoo is not a Hawk, a Conure is not an African Grey and so on and to treat any animal as interchangeable can leaves gaps or holes where the animals "mental pieces" don't quite fit together with what we've trained them to do. The Black Palm Cockatoo for example has a very unique mating practice where the male will beat a stick against the hollow log where it wishes to nest in order to attract a mate. The females are apparently attracted to the sound of this drumming which carries for many miles. No other Cockatoos perform this behavior. So if Cockatoos are behaving differently from other Cockatoos, how can we expect them to behave the exact same way as any other species of bird or expect them to behave in the same way as other types of animals such as cats and dogs? We all might learn the same way, but the truth is there is a species-specific difference that needs to be accounted for and this is only available through the study of Ethology.

But what is Ethology? Wildlife biologists studying birds (and other animals) in their native habitats compose collections of data known as Ethograms as they study the animals. These are very detailed accounts of the species-specific habits in the lives of parrots or other animals as they live day to day, month to month and year to year. As the Brelands stated in their treatise, "After 14 years of continuous conditioning and observation of thousands of animals, it is our reluctant conclusion that the behavior of any species cannot be adequately understood, predicted, or controlled without knowledge of its instinctive patterns, evolutionary history, and ecological niche". Any behavior we do not understand in our living rooms or on stage probably has its root in a naturally occurring behavior that the bird evolved to do over a period of millions or billions of years. As animal trainers or even people simply living with captive birds as pets it is our job to continually attempt to unravel the most complicated puzzles on the planet and I hope you enjoy the journey as much as I do.

As trainers we can change behavior but not instinct. I have always said that training is essentially a language that bridges the gap between the human and animal mind and Ethology can give us a glimpse into the world of our birds by telling us exactly how our birds lived and behaved in their native habitat. The gaps and holes in operant conditioning can be solved with this information, apply it to your birds and see for yourself. Try researching the everyday wild behaviors of the birds you share your lives with and you just might be surprised to see that the "odd" habit your bird does that you never understood is actually quite natural.

With all of that said, it is very important not to immediately attribute all problem behaviors to instinctive drift! The most common companion parrot problem-behaviors are *learned* behaviors. With parrots, in the debate of Nature vs. Nurture it is clear that Nurture is very much the winner. Biting and screaming parrots are the result of accidental training.

Just because your bird's species might have a reputation for behaving a certain way, such as being a good talker, being nippy, being a love sponge, or a screamer - that does NOT mean YOUR bird will act that way. Your bird is an INDIVIDUAL - Don't pigeonhole him into a category based on how other people's birds are behaving. I cringe every time somebody says something like "All Scarlet Macaws are nippy". —The truth is that that is a *generalization*. Generalizations are a fragmented thought process and it is not an accurate way to gauge how your bird should behave. This happens so often with birds such as African Greys. They are supposedly all amazing talkers with 400 word vocabularies right? Not always, some never even say one word. It is amazing how many behavior challenges get attributed to the fact that the bird is a certain 'type'. Well I am here to rip away that security blanket - I say no matter what you are told by someone you still need to put in the effort to make the change. Even if the birds "reputation" precedes him.

Every Interaction is a Training Session

Every interaction is a training session, whether you know it or not. Read that again if you have to until it sinks in. Every interaction is a training session. What do I mean by this? I mean every time you walk by the cage, or hold your bird, or pet your bird, or every time you feed your bird, or talk to your bird, every time, EVERY INTERACTION that you have with your bird your bird is learning. Every single person that owns a bird or even lives with a bird is a bird trainer. I don't care if you've never seen a clicker before or never even had a dedicated training session in your entire life - the fact is you are still interacting with your birds... and every interaction is a....? TRAINING SESSION! Very good! Even those of you that *do* have dedicated training sessions should take notice - after all, your bird doesn't just turn off his mind and millions of years of evolution to survive in a complex cause-and-effect world as soon as the session ends. We don't have to TRY to teach anything and yet we are still teaching. So what are you accidentally teaching your birds to do that you might not realize yet? Behavior problems are usually learned right? Birds aren't born knowing to scream for pizza crust right? Many birds do this though, and the behavior had to come from somewhere! Figure it out, the good, the bad, and the ugly, and figure out what you can do to send your bird the right message throughout the entire day, not just during dedicated training sessions. If you can do that this can be the most powerful training tip you will ever learn. This is one of the biggest pieces of my training philosophy. I hope it helps you the same way it has helped others in the past.

Developing Autonomy – A Note on Trick Training and Parrot Development

Bright lights above the stage, cameras flashing, the noise of the crowd, dazzling showgirls dancing on stage. You are one of the lucky few who has VIP tickets to the opening night of the newest and biggest show on the Las Vegas strip. The pyrotechnics are cued and with a deafening sound and a plume of smoke a flock of 9 free flying macaws soar above the crowd so close you could practically touch them, making it an interactive 3D experience that stimulates every one of your senses. Then as if by magic they fly to the entertainer on the stage and the show has only just begun...

The birds perform like precision instruments and you feel like they must have performed this thousands of times before, but that is yet another Las Vegas illusion and this is only the first night of the show.

How do we do it? How do we have our birds in newspapers, on television, on stage and on the big screen before their first birthday? The answer is simple; If you have read my blog before you know that ideally I begin training birds very young and that is no secret. The secret is that they can learn as soon as their eyes open and while many trainers aren't even working with their birds yet because they feel they are too young mine are already performing shows before they are fully weaned onto solid foods. Here I will give you my biggest trick to how I do what I do and why I do what I do. These techniques are working night after night, this is not a rehearsed DVD or presentation but training methods that actually have to work because the birds life might depend on how well it is trained. If you want a bird that flies outdoors you will not find anything that works better than this process of raising them from infancy to be Super Parrots. This is an A to Z guide to how I work with the birds from selecting them before birth to eventually performing in shows. I hope you enjoy the journey as much as I do.

Before Their Eyes Open
Many birds are chosen to do this before the even open their eyes for the

first time. Most of the birds I raise are special ordered and the owner is put on a waiting list so that even before the egg is laid there is a deposit on the bird and his destiny is already set in stone. Many of the birds come from my own pairs but if I don't have what a particular entertainer or show is looking for I get creative and start contacting my network of trusted breeders in an attempt to match the client with the perfect bird. The bird may come from Nevada, Arizona, California, Texas or Florida. Sometimes they are hatched in an incubator and raised from day one, other times they are left with the parents for 10 days-2 weeks until the eyes open. From here the number of feedings can be cut down from every few hours around the clock to 4 hand feedings per day but this usually happens around the time that the baby bird finally opens their eyes.

Normally I prefer not to be raising the bird at this time and instead I choose to leave the bird with the parents if at all possible. My typical feeding schedule when I take possession of the bird is 8a.m., 12p.m., 4p.m. and 8p.m. Before the eyes open the baby spends much of his time sleeping, pooping and eating. I believe they are becoming more aware of their surroundings every day because I have seen them respond to sounds as well as light (although at the time of hatching to the first ten days or so their eyes aren't even fully formed yet). I already usually have an idea of what tricks or behaviors the bird will be performing and I start getting the props and other items ready for later and planning the individuals training. At this time the main concerns we have besides cleanliness of course are warmth and food. If we can keep both of those needs met the bird will thrive. The bird is fed very small amounts several times per day and they are in a controlled temperature at all times.

The Locomotory Stage - You Don't Want To Miss It!
If you have read any of my independent research into their development or if you have seen an interview or other writings in the past you might have heard that this is the most crucial stage of development in my opinion. I recently had a Rosebreasted Cockatoo (also called a Galah) who was born on 5-10-2011. By July 26th she had been on TV, been in the Newspaper, she had performed in at least 3 shows, she had been

participating in my Featherpeudic pet therapy program and she was already flying free outdoors. She was NOT weaned yet and was still taking 1-2 feedings per day - That is what you can accomplish if you take advantage of the Locomotory Stage of development.

Many trainers disagree with training a bird that young and I respect many of them and their opinions/work but the evidence shows that the birds are investigating their environment and processing information - to me this is a sign that they are old enough to grasp cause and effect concepts. If you disagree that's fine, but you should know that while you are still twiddling your thumbs waiting for your birds to eat solid foods so you can begin training mine are already trick trained and talking "Super Parrots" entertaining crowds across the U.S.

At this age the birds eyes are open and they can move around at will. They are very food motivated and most babies will make a habit of chasing the syringe around begging for food even when their crops are so full they look like they are going to pop! This is perfect and it is exactly what you want. At this point I start holding the syringe an inch or so away and asking the bird to walk 1-2 steps to reach it. They usually don't mind! Just cue the bird and wait for them to come to the syringe. At first they might just reach out by stretching their necks, but after they get the picture you will have them crossing the living room in no time. This is how Merlin, one of my Macaws was trained. He was trained like the way I described above until eventually he was crossing the showroom of the Las Vegas casino he was going to be performing at.

During the Locomotory Stage I also teach the bird to Spin On Cue and Target. This translates directly to flight training skills later on if you shape the behaviors corectly. At this time the bird grows faster than at any other point in it's development, they normally become covered in down and pin-feathers begin to appear as the little creature starts looking more and more like a bird each day. They can get very vocal, in the wild it is normal to hear babies at this age several miles away from the nest. They are conscious for more and more time each day. Their instinctive behaviors are already hard-wired in place and it is common to see them preening themselves and their clutch mates and performing other natural behaviors.

Pre-Fledging Age: Before the First Flights
Before the bird is old enough to fly or even leave the warmth of the brooder at night the baby is actively engaged in exploring his or her environment and is playing with toys so I am already exposing them to props and beginning to work on other behaviors like gently bending their head down if I will be teaching them to do flips and somersaults or teaching other behaviors like waving on cue or shaking hands or rolling over on cue. I expose them to a large assortment of things besides props such as cameras, cables, lights, costume accessories and I have them interact with other animals for short periods of time so they become accustomed to this as well. If they will be working around pyrotechnics I use recordings of explosions and play them starting at a very low volume and gradually increasing the sound level with time.

It may seem like a lot but these birds are not as "spooky" or flighty as many others who do not go through all this preparation. I feel like a baby who has taken part in this "birdie boot camp" has a better toolbox than a second hand bird or even a standard baby who is trained later in life. I am not saying you cannot be successful when you are training such birds but I am indeed saying these birds who are raised in this way are superior when you are discussing performance parrots.

At this age the bird is awake for longer periods each day and actively seeks your companionship, many times they are fairly "clingy" during this time and the noise has risen dramatically. At this point they have usually associated you with food to such a degree that the mere sight of you will elicit a feeding response as they attempt to remind you again and again of their dependence on you. They are usually covered with feathers on 80%-90% of the body and are feeding around 2-3 times per day, eating larger and larger amounts of formula fewer times per day. Many birds such as Cockatoos may even weigh as much as their parents around this age. I am offering many foods to the bird even though they usually only chew it or pick at it without actually ingesting any of it. This is the beginning of the weaning stage. They can be performing several behaviors on cue by this time.

Weaning and Fledging Age
Now the bird is typically cut back to one feeding per day, but at first the bird is kept on 2 feedings per day and I feel the crop in the morning and at night to see if they are full and if I can get away with skipping a feeding. If the crop is full of seeds, pellets, peas and carrots or anything else I have offered them then I don't give them the feeding and I consider them on 1 feeding per day from then on but sometimes I go back and forth from 1 to 2 feedings for a few days so that the transition is gradual. Typically the bird takes his first flights to me right about when I cut them back to 1 feeding per day, I might still give them 2 feedings some days if they don't seem to be eating enough but they usually continue to beg for food even when they have some solid food in their crop.

When the bird is flapping around and thinking of flying to me I cue them and show the syringe as a lure, 9 times out of 10 they fly right to you, missing the target and crashing against your chest almost like a big hug. They are rewarded lavishly every time they fly to you, even if you didn't cue it. Flight training a baby is very informal at first and you are basically just encouraging them to perform the behavior. Flying is pretty unpredictable and it can take them a while to figure out the "brakes" but soon they get it and you have them flying to you each time you cue them with the syringe. If you remember how we trained them to come to you on cue earlier you will see that they have known how to perform this since a very early age, it was just the ground work that preceded the actual flying Recall.

The weaning stage is the most stressful part of raising a baby for me, because I am constantly wondering if they are eating enough and many time they might appear to be eating at a glance but in reality they are just hulling the seed etc and not actually ingesting the food. The birds are typically old enough to graduate to an actual cage instead of the brooder at night, enough feathers are covering their body now so they can thermoregulate properly. My birds typically take their first flights outdoors at this time, at first they are flown in aviaries and screened-in porches but soon I move them outdoors and they are flying free as they transition to the next stage.

The Post-Weaning Juvenile Stage
In the wild when a bird finally leaves the nest they are programmed to stay close to the parents, the behaviors and skills necessary for their survival are not inherited but rather learned through observation and the parents must teach them where to find water and food etc. This has no bearing on whether the animal is a K-type or R-type animal which many trainers feel is crucial to a birds success as a free-flying performance parrot. I do not agree, not only have I trained a flock of 200 breeder cockatiels to fly to me on cue (even though they had babies in the nest in some cases) it has been documented that even baby Budgerigars (Parakeets) stay with the father and continue to take feedings from him for about a week after they initially leave the nest. I use this natural "harness" to my advantage and I begin flying them outdoors without restraints or a creance and I rely solely on this natural tendency to stay close to the "parent". I have once been accused of "flight training with separation anxiety" because I do this but I do not feel that using natural behaviors in an effort to train a bird is in anyway harmful or detrimental to them. I am simply working with the bird's natural propensity to learn this behavior and I am there to shape it from the very beginning to create the exact result I am looking for.

I have found no better method to train birds to free fly outdoors and anytime a client or perspective parrot trainer asks me about flight training I point out that the best way is to train from infancy. Earlier we taught the bird to spin on cue, well now I shape the behavior so the bird is flying from Point A to Point A again in a circle. I Use the recall so the bird flies from Point A (a stand or perch) to Point B (myself). I also shape it so they fly from Point A to Point B back to Point A again. I then use the targeting behavior the bird has already learned to train him to fly from Point A to B to C because wherever the beak goes to touch the target the body will follow. I also begin using stair cases and apartment complexes as training grounds so the bird begins getting used to flying up and down and not just back and forth.

Many trainers say that the biggest problem they have is getting the bird to fly down from a tree or similar object and this is how you can go about flying the bird without the need to concern yourself with whether or not the bird will fly down to you if needed. I take this training further by having the bird fly to me from the top of a building and switching places so they are dropping vertically to me from rooftops and window sills. You can gradually increase the distance as much as you desire until they are flying to you from the top of a 400 foot tall casino if you desire.

Besides learning flight behaviors the birds are also learning how to eat solid foods exclusively and they are learning the finishing touches to whatever tricks they will be performing, such as card tricks or chained behaviors and so on. They really are super parrots at this time and it is always hard emotionally to send them to their new home and new life as a performance parrot. We begin exposing them to the "set" or wherever they will be performing and get them comfortable in that environment. I do get a level of satisfaction beyond that of raising a typical bird because it is a great feeling to know the bird will be entertaining people from around the world, and besides that I know they will have a great life living in a mansion and performing in world class shows such as Cirque Du Soliel. It is plenty of hard work to raise any baby bird, but it is always worth it and I plan on raising performance parrots for quite some time and continuing to experiment with the learning abilities of neonates.

Quality Over Quantity

Instead of getting 20, or 30, or 40 "ok" or *decent* repetitions, I'd rather get 3 or 4 AMAZING reps. Get a few good reps done and then quit while you are ahead - Keep it short and end the sessions on a good note BEFORE the bird starts "shutting down" on you (If you go until the bird becomes unresponsive your sessions are TOO LONG). If your bird starts slowing down pack it in and close it down. We should be aiming for a consistent state of motivation and receptivity throughout the entire day - not just during your training sessions. Too often we "burn them out" and use up all the birds motivation, leaving us with a bird that doesn't comply when we really do need it (such as when we need them to step down off of a shoulder, or enter the cage or travel carrier willingly, or return to us from a very tall place they've flown to, etc). There is no race to be won, birds live a long time in most cases so what's the rush? Even if you just teach your bird 4 tricks per year - in 10 years your bird will know over 40 tricks! That is more than several birds combined will perform in most bird shows! And many people that train their birds accomplish MUCH more than just 4 tricks per year going at only a very slow pace. So remember: Take your time, aim for quality over quantity, and keep the sessions short.

The author free-flying one of his hand-raised Rose Breasted Cockatoos. This bird regularly performs in free-flight bird shows and is capable of amazing flying displays. Flight training should only be attempted under the guidance of an experienced trainer.

A Note on Clickers

I often see people talking about clicker training on the internet and many times people don't quite understand what a clicker is exactly, for example, I just read a post where someone wanted to learn more about using clickers to train a hawk for falconry. The answer he got was simply to click whenever the animal did something correctly....but clickers by themselves are NOT supposed to be a reward - They are a communication tool that is supposed to be PAIRED with rewards. Clicks by themselves aren't good enough to motivate an animal; it has to mean something positive to the animal. He has to want more clicks because "clicks are good" in his experience. Another common thing I see being taught about clickers is that they tell the animal when it did something right and bridges the gap between when the animal did the desirable behavior when a treat is given - This is actually correct, but it is only a very basic description and it is NOT the only thing a clicker does. A clicker actually helps me communicate with an animal and achieve results in several different ways:

First of all, you don't need a clicker to "clicker train" an animal. You can use something like a verbal response such as "good" in the exact same way you would use a clicker - but the problem with that is that many people tell their birds that they are "Good birds" all the time and treats don't always come afterwards. With clickers (or any other bridging stimulus) the rewards have to come EVERY TIME THE ANIMAL HEARS IT or else the clicker will be meaningless to the animal. Many people train their animals without a clicker and do a wonderful job - but you have to make sure that the substitute isn't something that the bird will hear all the time. It has to be some very specific auditory, visual, or tactile signal that is ONLY used as a bridging stimulus.

Many people also believe that you need to "condition the animal to the clicker" and I have seen many new (and even experienced) trainers refuse to use them because they believed that you have to do separate training sessions BEFORE you could even train the animal. They think you have to train him to be trained. But this is NOT true. You do not have to have separate sessions only dedicated to teaching the bird that "clicks mean treats". Doing so is just a waste of time. Just pick up the clicker and go - you will see for yourself that they become "conditioned" straight away.

Clickers are very precise so the primary use for clickers is as an event marker (telling the animal the exact time that it did something correctly). But as we've already discussed it also bridges the gap between when he or she performed correctly and when a reward is given (It might take me a second or two to go into my pocket and pull out a treat - but the animal should know that treats ALWAYS come when he hears a click so the clicker has already communicated that a treat is on the way. This means it is ok if it takes me a second or two to get the reward out of my pocket). But it doesn't ONLY tell the bird that food is on the way, since it is a precise event marker it allows us to shape behaviors by very small approximations and get closer and closer to our goals with each repetition (for example, many people have played the "warmer/colder" game or "Marco Polo", and the clicker works in the same way as these games and lets us tell him or her that he/she is "warmer", or closer to the desired behaviors). This "game" allows us to increase the prerequisite behaviors required to earn a treat ("hmm, I got rewarded for lifting my foot this high last time, but this time I lifted it the same height and didn't get rewarded....should I try lifting it higher"? CLICK "Oh ok, I was supposed to lift my foot higher"). By increasing the requirements little by little I eventually reach my desired goal and the bird is roller skating, or flying to me, etc.

Another thing that clickers can be used for that I NEVER see discussed is telling the animal WHEN I expect the behavior to be performed after he is cued (or asked) to do it - this is just another part of the "warmer cooler game". Exactly how long of a time frame does the animal have to comply with my request and complete the desired behavior after he is asked and still be rewarded? Well that is up to you but you have to communicate this amount of time to the animal - how do you communicate that? By using the clicker to tell him how long the window of opportunity is open. This is just an example but if I call the bird to fly down from a tree but he dawdles for 20 minutes before finally returning I am not going to reward him. That is too much latency for me. If I was doing a 30 minute bird show I can't wait 20 minutes for the bird to decide to fly down to me. Or if a hawk suddenly flew into the area I would need the bird to return to me much sooner than 20 minutes after I asked him. We have to condition the bird so that he understands that he only has a certain amount of time in order to perform the different behaviors or else the window of opportunity will close. Since the clicker is so precise it is the perfect tool for this job. (By the way If you are continually having problems with excessive latency or very delayed responses to your cues the common causes are lack of motivation/receptivity or even more commonly it is poor training strategies in general.)

On the other side of the coin there are instances when we need to extend the time that the animal needs to do a specific behavior before he has earned the treat. For example, I often see pet owners make a giant mistake when training their dog to sit - they get the dog to do the behavior 3 or 4 times and then all of the sudden they expect him to stay for an hour! It doesn't work like that. You have to shape the behavior like we discussed earlier. At first you are rewarding him just for sitting on cue, but as time goes on you increase the time that his butt must stay on the grass before he earns the reward. Wait 2 seconds, then click and reward. Then 3 seconds. Then 5 seconds, and so on. Slow and steady wins the race.

Another basic example of the use of clickers is to find positive solutions to problems that the owners had previously punished the animal for doing. Let's use dog owners as an example again: When attempting to potty train the dog, the most common way people attempt to do this is by flogging the animal and rubbing his/her nose in the "mess" when they "go" inside the house. But there are more positive solutions. What I like to do is use clickers and treats and catch the animal doing something RIGHT, instead of punishing him for doing something wrong. It is a much more positive approach to take the dog outside after a large meal, to a designated area, and wait for him to "go". When he does click and reward. Repeat this for a while and you not only have a dog that goes potty outside but he goes in ONE SPECIFIC SPOT so the owner doesn't have to collect piles all over the whole yard for an hour or 2 every week. He can just go outside with a shovel and in one or 2 scoops clean an entire weeks worth of "mess". So clickers can help us find more ethical solutions that are better for everyone involved.

Quick Fix Training Methods

If you have a problem with your bird's behavior and are seeking advice - run away from "quick fix" remedies. We live in a world where instant gratification is king and this attitude is increasingly finding its way into animal training...but not for the better of our companion and show animals. For example, I just saw a post on a parrot board where somebody said they had a hard time getting their bird to stay on the play-stand outside his cage. A lady that has owned birds for over 30 years told him to put a "loud colored feather duster" on the floor so that hopefully the bird would be frightened of this object and remain on his perch. Another example I have seen recently is a bird owner was instructed by a "bird expert" to chase the bird with a R/C car when it screamed, and if that didn't work they were instructed to forcefully attack the bird with a towel, wrap him up, throw him in a travel carrier, and leave him in a dark closet for an indeterminate period of time....does anybody else see anything wrong with this?

While it may take longer, it IS possible to make the animal WANT to do whatever it is that we want him to do - and actually completely and totally 100% by his choice. Think about it like this: Most people find their way to work on time each and every day. Why is this? Because their behavior is rewarded with paychecks that they can use to buy food, pay for housing, take care of the family, and so on. Just like the humans that find their way to situations that prove "rewarding", our animals CAN learn that certain behaviors like staying on the play-stand or doing a different vocalization is rewarding. They find their way to the behaviors that are beneficial for them to do, just like we do. Yes it might take longer to get results sometimes but it is worth it and it is the *right way* to do it.

A Note on "Schedule"

In contrast to what many other parrot "experts" say, I do not believe in having your bird on too strict of a schedule. If you have dedicated training times and so forth that is fine, but some people take this way too far. I believe the parrot owners (and especially African Grey owners it seems) who have every little detail planned down to the last neurotic detail are training the birds to be afraid of or unaccustomed to change. They are creating rescue birds.

Have You "Tried Everything" To Solve A Problem Behavior?

When people tell me that they have tried everything to change their birds behavior, they might have tried plenty of things but usually they don't give it enough time to actually see results. The other question is whether or not all those training attempts were using quality science-based methods, or did the tip, trick, or technique come from a chatroom or one of those bird training websites that market misinformation? You see, when it comes time to modify a problem behavior in a captive parrot you have to arm yourself with the best, most up to date information available...otherwise you will oftentimes realize that the problem has gotten worse. And when you DO find quality information, treat it that way. Give it the time that it needs to work.

Is My Bird a Boy or Girl?

I can't tell you how many times I have heard someone say something along the lines of "My bird is a girl because she likes men" or "I think Polly is a male because when he talks he sounds like a boy"....This is NOT an accurate way to determine your birds gender! These things are learned - Not determined by your birds' sex. If your bird prefers interacting with one gender over another that could be because of something as simple as what gender human he was raised by, or it could be because of something as simple as a bad experience with the opposite gender human, and the bird is transferring that association over to another human. There are plenty of reasons why a bird might prefer one gender over another - but that does NOT have anything to do with what gender the BIRD is. Thirty years ago most birds seemed to prefer women, because more women were raising birds. And even Wild-Caughts usually preferred women because they were always captured in the wild by male poachers. So just because your bird likes men or women more, or sounds like a man or a woman, that doesn't reveal his or her gender - if that were the case all my birds that mimicked a cat, dog, or rooster must not have been parrots!

Ok here is the next part to this: Any time I tell people this stuff it seems like clockwork that they will soon say something like "Well, I don't care about what gender my bird is. Why should I care? I am not going to breed him". Ok, you might not intend to produce a bunch of tiny Polly parrots, but it is absolutely important to know what gender your bird is. Why? Say for example you come home one day and find Polly lying limp on the bottom of the cage - something is wrong! The cause can be many, many, MANY things. Wouldn't it be advantageous to know for a FACT that it is NOT egg-binding for example, a common cause of death in female psittacines? Knowing the gender can help rule out potential health problems and help the vet reach a decision faster at a time where time is literally the difference between life and death. The same "presenting symptoms" can be caused by drastically different problems depending on the birds gender - and in this case as well as any other, knowledge is power.

A Note on Hormones

While it may be 'convenient' to do so, stop blaming aggression or other behavior problems on something like 'hormones'. The typical Facebook post goes something like this: "Oh, my bird just bit the crap out of me - he's hormonal". Every time I see this I think really? Are you sure? How are you sure? Do you have blood tests confirming such? Where is your paperwork from the vet? It couldn't be ANY other cause? Have you identified other potential causes and systematically eliminated them until your hormone conclusion was all that remained? Or are you just GUESSING??? Guessing gets you nowhere. Assigning blame to something you can't really change gets you nowhere. But it's 'convenient' and so we do it. It is more convenient than doing some digging, figuring out what is *really* going on, figuring out what you need to do to change your situation, then implementing your training strategies and STICKING TO IT. Even if something like 'hormones' ARE at work they are NOT the sole cause of your current challenge with Polly. Saying that it is is either inexperience, lack of education, or just plain copping out in my experience. The LAST thing you should do is attribute your bird's behavior to an immutable higher power that you are helpless in the face of. You CAN make a difference....if you are willing to do the work. You own the bird - own the problems, even if you didn't cause them in the first place.

Say "No" To No

The trick to training birds and other companion animals with positive reinforcement successfully is REWARDING "GOOD" BEHAVIORS & IGNORING "BAD" BEHAVIORS.

It might sound simple but there still tends to be some confusion. When I say we ignore unwanted behaviors - that means we do not "correct" the animals with negative stimuli. We do not berate them, we do not yell, we do not hit, we don't "get even", we don't "get after them", we don't pinch the toe, we don't spray them with a water bottle, we don't Say "no". We say "No" to no and catch them doing something right instead. So please, say "no" to no.

A Quick Tip for Talking

Put some kind of label or sign on your bird's cage to help with speech training. Even if it is just a Post-it Note on your bird's cage with a few phrases, the birds name, etc., this can help more than you might realize. People from all corners of the world know that parrots have the ability to mimic human speech and so most people naturally try to get parrots to talk when they see them. So if you have something on the cage that says: "Hi my name is Cappy, I say: "Walk The Plank" you will have guests saying that choice phrase to your bird and therefore he will hear it spoken much more often than if you were to just try to teach him to talk during dedicated training sessions. Every interaction is a training session remember? So take charge of what your bird will be learning when he interacts with people passing by his cage. Another benefit to doing this is that your bird will hear the word(s) or phrases spoken in a variety of different voices, tones, accents etc. Once you get your bird(s) saying some fun things it is VERY easy to put it all on cue, so that the bird says the words and phrases when you want him to say it.

Is it "Cool" To Have A "One Person Bird"?

So many people are "proud" to have birds that ONLY THEY can handle, interact with, etc. That is NOT something to be proud of and we should try to avoid having "one person birds". What happens if your "one person bird" outlives you? What happens if he bites someone severely enough that medical attention is required (I'll give you a hint: It starts with "A" and ends with "nimal control citation"....)? What happens when this relationship alienates your spouse or other family members because no matter how hard he/she tries they can't even feed the bird without the possibility of stitches?

Yes many species of psittacines naturally tend to be more "monogamous" - but not all of them, not all of the time, and even those that ARE can LEARN to interact politely with others. We are HUMANS, NOT BIRDS, we do not make good "mates" for a parrot! So foster a trainer/student relationship instead of a mate/pair relationship. Don't let the bird's species be an excuse for unhealthy behaviors either! They act the way they do because for one reason or another it is to their advantage to behave that way (just like we humans do)...I often see statements such as "African Greys are one person birds" - but there are Greys that interact with new people/other members of the household all day, so that statement is not accurate. The truth is that each individual bird has been conditioned to behave the way it does. I'll say that again: Conditioned. It's not because the bird has "mistaken identity", or "doesn't know it's a bird", it's because it can really make people feel good about themselves and boost their ego to have a bird that acts this way (or people unknowingly/accidentally reinforced the behavior). But it is NOT the best thing for the bird. Humans find their way to situations and behaviors that are advantageous (such as arriving to work at 6am on Thursday), birds do this too. It's just that they are arriving to the "wrong place" and behaving in a way that conflicts with sustainable bird keeping.

One more point - We need to remember that there are people that don't want us owning companion birds (or any other animal) and they point to this exact type of "problem" as an example of why we shouldn't keep them as pets - so next time you see someone bragging about their bird that only the can handle - thank them for perpetuating a myth that could one day lead to your bird(s) being taken from you!

The author teaching a Hyacinth Macaw to "wave" on cue.

Understanding the Noise

One of the most common complaints I hear parrot owners mention when they talk about their birds is the noise level. From Conures to Cockatoos there can sometimes be a little more volume than a new owner bargained for when they first introduced a new ball of feathers into their lives. Of course the ideal parrot owner would have researched the characteristics of the particular bird they were planning to share their lives with before bringing the new addition home but I myself have dealt with issues people had who supposedly read everything that had ever been written about their particular bird and they were so sure it was the right bird for them when they brought it home.

The first identification we need to make about screaming is an observation anyone who has ever visited these animals in the wild can attest to – These animals are naturally very loud! Simply spend 5 minutes in their native range and you will agree. Float down the Amazon river and I promise you will hear many of the birds long before you ever see them, spend some time with the Cockatoos in Australia and you will be amazed that anyone ever considered them for life in an apartment - So when you are dealing with a bit more noise than you bargained for simply realize that this is normal and natural.

THE 5 MAIN TYPES OF PROBLEM VOCALIZATIONS
There are several reasons why your bird may be screaming its head off, I will list them here in no particular order and I will attempt to give my perspective on the subject for each reason.

1. NATURAL OR CYCLICAL VOCALIZATION
This is the vocalization that will happen on a daily basis. A perfect example of this type of vocalization is the noise that many birds display at dawn and dusk. This behavior has been documented in most birds that were studied in their natural habitat and while there may be exceptions you can expect almost any larger species of parrot to take part in this daily routine.

2. CONTACT CALLS

This is a very common habit for birds who have adapted this behavior as a means of surviving the harsh environments they are originally from. A contact call is a form of communicating between at least 2 birds (usually a bonded pair) but the unfortunate aspect of this vocalization for many pet owners is the fact that a human can be substituted for another bird if your parrot is sufficiently bonded to you. Normally the bird will vocalize to his or her mate (natural or perceived) and the bird would ideally receive a response from its partner if everything was ok. The problem here is when the bird views his owner as a mate and the owner cannot dedicate themselves to the bird 24 hours per day due to the fact that they usually have employment and families (which the bird cannot compete with). This leads to high levels of Separation Anxiety for the bird who calls and calls but receives no reply. In the wild this would usually mean their mate had perished and is it any wonder they get so upset?! This vocalization can be very persistent and as the bird gets more and more frustrated the volume can almost always be expected to increase.

3. VOCALIZING FOR SELF AMUSEMENT

The parrot family is well known for their ability to mimic human speech as well as an infinite number of other noises. In fact this ability is one of the most endearing qualities of our birds in captivity and one of the main reason so many people share their lives with a bird. Spend a few minutes with a group of Macaws (or almost any other birds) in the wild or in captivity and you will notice the occasional squawk, chirp, whistle etc., sometimes they feel the need entertain themselves and this is the category for this type of vocalization. Many times when the bird is exhibiting this behavior when you are not specifically training him or her the cause is boredom.

4. HYPERACTIVE VOCALIZATION

Have you ever seen a Cockatoo in over drive, jumping up and down, crest up, screaming his head off? We call this Hyperactive Vocalization because it is the product of overstimulation. This is associated with higher levels of adrenaline and/or other hormones coursing through the birds bloodstream – almost any experienced bird keeper knows that their birds get "loud and rowdy" during the breeding season and this is just one of many forms of vocalizing your bird will make that can be considered Hyperactive Vocalization. It can come from excitement, stress or any other event which causes the bird to operate on "auto pilot".

5. MANIPULATIVE SCREAMING

It has been discovered that certain types of birds are intelligent enough to realize their actions can influence the actions of other animals. This is particularly interesting from a scientific viewpoint because this behavior suggests an awareness of self which is not a credit that animals other than humans are given at this time. Cockatoos and Corvids such as Ravens are the best known for this behavior but in a nut shell this basically means the bird knows that he can get a specific result if he acts in a certain way. The bird is rewarded for his actions (usually unintentionally) and this habit becomes reinforced. I call this "Cause and Effect Behavior" and essentially what is happening when your bird is displaying this behavior is that he is the one training you. It is very easy to fall victim to this trap, the bird screams and you are making an important business call so you run right over and give him a treat to shut him up. Big mistake! This is just one of thousands of scenarios that this behavior can rear its ugly head - the point is to not react to any undesirable behavior. There are always solutions if you stop and think through the problem. Why not give the bird a bath before you make the phone call? Then he will be busy preening and you solved the problem without any negative reinforcement.

REMEDIES

If your bird is displaying any of the behaviors mentioned earlier just relax, take a deep breath and know that everything will be ok. No matter how many people tell me they have tried everything the truth is that they might very well be at their wits end, but they did not truly "try everything". Give the solution a chance before giving up and moving on to the next one, it will always take time and patience but in the end it is always worth it. As I stated earlier certain birds will be louder than others and it is up to you to do the research long before you ever bring a bird home, educate yourself as much as possible and be truly honest about what you are getting yourself into. Always remember that "an ounce of prevention is worth a pound of cure", so it might not be a good idea to have a Mollucan Cockatoo in your apartment (actually it's a terrible idea). The following is a list of suggestions that have worked for me in the past with several birds of varying species and problematic screaming behaviors.

Don't Punish
For some reason it is very common for people to spray the bird with a water bottle as punishment for screaming. Any punishment will severely damage the trust of your bird who has evolved much differently from the domesticated animals we are so used to seeing corrective actions being taken with (for example, the dog urinates on the carpet so the owner pushes his nose into the mess and then verbally reprimands the animal as well). This is Negative Reinforcement or as I like to call it "Escape Avoidance Training" and it is a very poor training system that yields very poor results. Besides that, many of the parrots we live with come from places where water is very abundant so it is both physically and mentally necessary for the bird to bathe. When they are taught to fear taking baths the seeds have been sewn for quite a few problems such as FDB's (Feather Destructive Behaviors).

Sound Proofing
As we learned earlier, screaming is natural for many birds. It is a great idea to have at least one place that the bird can "go nuts" without causing any problems. After all, many birds get the loudest when they are happy so it needs to be ok for them to be loud sometimes.

Take The Bird With You When Possible
This works great for Contact Calling, of course the bird can't go everywhere you do but it can lessen the amount of stress the bird has. If he can see you, hear you etc he won't be freaking out because you are gone will he? In extreme cases of over-bonding where the bird is considerably unhealthy and/or unstable mentally because he is so

attached to you it may be time to consider the addition of another bird. Parrots are way too social to live in isolation.

Channel Vocalization into Speech Training

Another solution to Contact Calling is to find an acceptable alternative that the bird can do which doesn't result in being evicted from your home. Find another word or phrase that works for you and start saying it to the bird all the time. Then try using it when you leave the room but try to do the word or sound before the bird does so that you are the one initiating this behavior and not the other way around.

Ignore Unwanted Behavior and Reward Desired Behavior

This is the secret to solving Manipulative Screaming and is self explanatory. Show absolutely no reaction when the bird is attempting to manipulate you.

Arrange For a Friend or Relative to Stop by

Great for the bird that is regularly experiencing Separation Anxiety and behaving as a result to this form of stress, it is usually easier than it seems to have somebody stop by and check up on your bird when you are gone for several hours at a time.

Environmental Stimulation

Busy beaks can't scream so keep the cage loaded with toys, treats and anything else that will keep your bird busy. Soft music can really help to calm the bird down and hiding treats can be a great way to tap into the birds natural foraging instincts which will keep him busy. There is a phenomenon in the training world called Contra Free Loading and it is scientifically proven that a bird (or other animal) will work for food even when there is a full bowl right next to it.

Control Environmental Triggers

Certain things such as the length of daylight in a 24 hour period can really have an impact on your birds behavior because they are so "in tune" with the seasons. Much like plants that know that it is time to flower at a certain time of year or go into stasis at another time, birds reproductive cycles are closely linked to the cycles of the seasons. If the bird is receiving more than 12 hours of light per day it will enter breeding mode if it is the correct age and this means the volume will go up. Shortening the days can really help you improve your situation.

Give The Bird A "Work Out"

A training session can really help you to get rid of some extra energy the bird has and many times a Trick Trained bird has many times fewer problems than those birds who receive no training on a regular basis. If a trained bird ever shows an undesired behavior they can be redirected by performing a simple trick such as targeting or spinning on cue. Training Sessions are best used proactively to combat screaming. If you know your bird will sound-off at 6pm give him an intensive and tiring session before then.

Let the Bird "Cool Off"

When you first come home or when a bird is displaying body language associated with overstimulation I advise you to not run over to the bird right away. When they act up or give you signs through the use of their body language just wait for a better time to interact with him or her.

Recognize What "Sets the Bird Off"

Know your bird and realize what triggers the problem behaviors in your pet – then act on it. Observance is key and your patience will be rewarded. If the bird screams when you eat your meals then don't eat in front of him etc.

Time Out

When the bird screams show absolutely no reaction, make no eye contact; don't even make any indication that you hear the noise. The only acceptable action I would ever advise that someone to take that could even come close to being described as a punishment is a time out, which all it consists of is calmly getting up, and walking away when the bird screams. Don't leave it isolated for long periods of time either, when the bird stops screaming you can go back and praise it. The secret here is not to just ignore unwanted behavior but to catch the bird being a good boy or girl and praise it lavishly!

Taking Skills to a Higher Level

The best trainers in the world all have one thing in common: They make it look easy. No matter how educated someone may become in the theories and methods it takes to train parrots there is still a mechanical aspect or skill that is just as crucial to your success. After so many times of teaching a particular behavior a kind of "muscle memory" develops that is much like a musician who has played the same chord or piece of music over and over until practice has made perfect. They can literally "do it in their sleep". To become a master musician, a person practices scales or "runs" in order to sharpen their reflexes and make their instrument more of a part of themselves. This article is just a few "scales" for you to practice that will help bring your training to the next level. Now, go create your masterpiece!

LESSON 1: Get Clicking!
While there have been many amazing trainers such as Tani Robar who achieved wonderful results without ever using a clicker, the fact is that they are a modern tool which has forever changed training as we know it. These are the most recent "limb" in the evolution of training animals of all species, from horses to dogs to tigers and elephants to penguins etc. They are so useful because clickers allow you to shape a behavior little by little, small approximation by small approximation until you have birds doing amazing feats such as flying circles over an audience, doing card tricks or navigating through the most complex obstacle course. Whenever I am training new birds for a show in Las Vegas I use clickers on a daily basis to shape these intricate behaviors until the birds are precision instruments. The best way to practice clicking is to play a game with your friends and see if you can "train" them to perform a task such as opening the front door or making you a sandwich. Think of a relatively simple task and all the actions that are required to complete your "trick". Soon you will realize that even a "simple" task like fetching a glass of water isn't so simple after all! You may decide it is easier to start at the end of the behavior to train your specific task or it might be better to start at the beginning. Ask yourself that question BEFORE you are actually training because sometimes it makes things much easier to start at the ending,

while other times it is more appropriate to start at the beginning. Practice holding Chopsticks or other items you may use as Targets in the same hand as the clicker, when you get comfortable with that you can move up to holding the clicker, a targeting stick AND a treat... you never know when this will come in handy but trust me, when you need this ability you will be glad you worked on it ahead of time!

LESSON 2: Put Down The Clicker And Food Rewards!
Ok, now you probably think I am crazy since I just told you to practice using a clicker because they can be so helpful... but to be a successful trainer you must be versatile and it is a wonderful thing to "go old school" with your training by verbally marking the progress instead of using a clicker. Conditioning a bird to use a clicker is an entire lesson in itself, so when you are faced with a deadline to have something trained you don't want to waste time. What if you are 10 minutes late for a training session before you even leave the house but then you get stuck in traffic, miss your exit on the freeway AND can't find a place to park at the casino you are working at that day? Oh I forgot the best part: You left your clicker at home! Now I'd like to take a moment to give you some very good advice, ALWAYS HAVE AN EXTRA CLICKER IN YOUR CAR!!! If you are training for a living or you are showing your birds professionally be sure to keep an extra in each pair of pants that you own, in the glove box, hanging on the rearview mirror, dangling from a keychain and everywhere else you can think of. Do that and I promise you will only be left stranded without a clicker a handful of times per year. Even if you do find yourself at a gig without a clicker it's ok because you listened to my advice and tried this exercise. Maybe it's me but I swear those things have little legs you can't see and they have a habit of running away as soon as you set them down. Don't say I didn't warn you. The other part of this lesson is to find ways to motivate a trainee without food motivation. I have met birds that will work their little butts off for clapping, verbal praise, a touch on the chest or head, petting, my cell phone, water bottles, lotion bottles, a favorite toy, mirrors and so on. We call these types of reinforcers Secondary Reinforcers or Learned Reinforcers. These are play and social interests that the bird sees as valuable and you will be surprised at how motivated

the right bird can become by something as simple as a water bottle. Besides that, it's awesome to see other trainers jaws hang open when they see you being successful with this. My favorite part of working with Secondary Reinforcers is that it really gets you thinking like a trainer – different birds will see different things as valuable and each bird is a unique individual.

LESSON 3: Write a Training Plan
A training plan is a step by step guide you write for yourself detailing every action you will take to complete your goal and train the desired behavior. I really suggest you give this a try for every animal and every behavior you train. Really go into detail and figure out what you are going to do and how you are going to do it. Think about what you are looking for the animal to do before you move on to the next step, for example if you are training a bird to spin on cue you will begin by teaching it to turn only half way at first. You will write something like "begin by giving your cue and moving a treat behind the birds' ear or behind his back to tempt the animal into turning half-way. It will be slow when you start, but eventually the bird gets the idea and you build up momentum, going faster and faster with each repetition. Eventually when the bird turns right away, you catch him directly after he turns and move the treat behind his ear again so he completes a full 360 rotation before he gets the treat from then on. From here you phase out the lure by moving your hand back and making the cue less exaggerated with each repetition". Make it thorough and precise and stick to the plan. Do this every time and soon you will be doing it in your head and even innovating as you move along, like putting natural behaviors on cue as you come across them. This process really makes you think like a trainer. You can prepare yourself mentally for real-world scenarios by figuring out a training plan in advance well before you come across the bird you will be training, and then put your hypothesis to the test when you come across a real situation where you can try it out. Also try to do this with solving problem behaviors such as biting or with tricks like saying a specific word on cue.

LESSON 4: Take a Class
Learning from a professional who has done this for several years can really improve your game. Many of the best hold seminars once per year at the very least. The problem with trainers is that the best ones are usually the hardest to come in contact with, beware of internet "know-it-alls" who you meet in chat rooms because many of them aren't as great as they think they are, despite their good intentions. Many times the advice they give out has no basis in scientific fact and can actually do more harm than good. Ask for references before trusting any advice. I'm not trying to be mean I just want you to protect you and your birds from harm and heartbreak because there is plenty of misinformation out there online. Barbara Heidenreich, Steve Martin and Chris Biro are all trainers other than myself who do this every day and offer training classes, seminars, workshops or other methods of training materials that can be trusted and will not result in accidentally training the bird to fear you or risk bodily harm to the parrot. These people have a wealth of information that can serve you well and will set you on the path to training success. I highly recommend each one that I listed. I also give training classes to help you get the most from your birds but they fill up fast so be sure to sign up and save your seat early!

LESSON 5: Take On Multiple Birds
There are certain times of the year when I am expected to work with a dozen birds or more per day and the ability to take on multiple "students" can not only keep you on your toes and test your skills and flexibility, but it can also make your life much easier when you have daunting tasks to perform such as the time when I had to train every parrot in a sanctuary to step up on cue. This is very fast paced but there is no better way to hone your training "reflexes". You will get to a point where certain things happen automatically after a while of doing this, even though every bird is different there is the mechanical aspect of training that I mentioned earlier and you will get more comfortable and confident with every bird you work with. Start with 2 or 3 birds and train something easy like the "turn around". If you get comfortable doing this then move up a bird at a time until you are doing 5-6 at a time. When this becomes natural to you

and you can pull it off without any problems you are ready to give demonstrations at local bird clubs etc.

LESSON 6: Test Yourself

If there is ever a behavior you feel like you might not be able to train because it seems too hard for you then you have just found a weak point to your training and you should seriously consider giving it a try anyway. I was just at a seminar another trainer was giving in Hollywood and she was pretty good, but after her presentation ended she spent quite some time asking me about how I flight train the birds to free fly outdoors and dive off of casinos etc., after a while she admitted that even though she had studied under an amazing teacher she felt that training flight was too complicated and she was not skilled enough to take on such a complex set of behaviors. I told her that it really is quite simple and that birds were designed to fly so she needed to stop thinking it was such a difficult thing because almost any bird will fly without any training whatsoever! She was limiting herself with the way she was thinking and even though she could train complex behaviors she didn't want to take on the most natural behavior a bird can perform! Do not limit yourself with your way of thinking, if you can think it up you can most likely teach a parrot to perform it. I actually saw a trainer teach a Tortoise to target on cue and if we can teach a simple animal like a tortoise we can definitely make something happen with an animal as intelligent as a parrot! Another thing many trainers do is make excuses as to why a behavior cannot be trained instead of figuring out how to do it. The lady who gave the seminar began to do this by saying it was dangerous to flight train some birds and the truth is that it can be very safe to train a bird to do this indoors if you take the necessary precautions. You can even begin teaching this to a bird who is currently clipped. I don't believe every bird should be allowed free-flight outdoors but this can be done safely indoors with many birds. The trainer then spent a bit more time asking about the way I train and guess what? After 15 years of training animals professionally she is attempting to train flight. She just needed to believe in herself, I hope you will too!

Flight Training Philosophy

Parrots have been kept in captivity for thousands of years. From ancient Egyptian kings to Roman emperors, even bloodthirsty pirates were enchanted by the grace and beauty of birds. Alexander the Great was well known for carrying a parakeet wherever he went and the distant cousins of his bird still carry that history with them in their common name: "The Alexandrine Parakeet". Queen Isabella of Spain was presented with a pair of Scarlet Macaws as a gift upon Christopher Columbus's return from the New World. Wherever you look you will see birds in our collective history no matter how far back you search. And for all these years the majority of birds we kept had their wings clipped.

The issue of humans having "dominion" over animals can be traced back to religious ideology, we are taught that we are "superior" and thus we can impose our will upon the animal kingdom (with force if necessary).

Many people are opposed to the idea of allowing a parrot to fly outdoors and I feel that the majority of the opposition comes from the simple belief system many people have that we have to force animals to do things. Many people feel that allowing an animal choice and unrestricted freedom to exercise that choice is harmful. This is what I call the "Dog On A Leash Concept". It is interesting to me to realize how many people simply cannot grasp the concept of allowing an animal to choose its own actions. I am not talking about a total lack of safe boundaries or even a set of "rules" but instead I am talking of the animal being allowed to do whatever it wants, except that it wants to do what we ask it to do. I am talking about compliance and communication, not force or coercion.

If you are giving a presentation to a crowd and the bird flies off 80 feet to the top of a tree what do you do? Do you stop the show, start panicking and call the fire department to come rescue the bird? No, the bird comes down to you willingly because it wants to do what you want it to do!

There are several people out there flying their birds outdoors. Most of us do not advocate or suggest that just anybody let their bird fly free, but instead we just smile and nod when we see another person other than ourselves talking about the subject. In fact, MOST people should not try this at home because they lack the commitment and dedication required to do this safely. If the average person can't even teach a canine simple obedience cues then how can they be expected to do everything required to live with a flighted parrot? The truth is, not every bird and every trainer/owner has what it takes and many companion birds would be better off clipped for safety's sake like the people we mentioned who kept birds for the past several generations. Flight training is very rewarding but it is all or nothing - 100% or 0%. Train the bird hard like a Drill Sergeant at boot camp or just let it be the snugly little "perch potato" who brightens your day when you come home from work. I have birds that dive off of casinos in Las Vegas and I have some that are clipped. It does not have to be the polarizing subject it currently is where people either say you are a barbaric person because you clip the bird or you are reckless and care nothing for their safety if you allow them flight. It is a choice, it is an important one but it is one that you must make alone and don't worry about what the people in chatrooms or online communities say, the majority of these people are hardly experts and there is a plethora of misinformation out there on the internet.

But isn't it "dangerous"?

The truth is: Yes, it is dangerous, in fact if you read anything that I have written about the subject of flight I talk about that first. To better explain my stance on parrot safety I will tell you a story about a Mini Macaw named "Baby". Baby was my bird, she was a Chestnut Fronted Macaw I got at weaning age and she was probably the best bird I will ever have. She was my best friend. Then one day I came home from working all day and her swing was hanging funny in her cage and she hadn't eaten the food I had left in the morning. The swing was specifically made for pet birds yet she had ingested one of the little bolts that held it together and died. There was nothing that could be done.

So if you can understand that something as simple as a bird toy specifically made for pet birds can kill your bird you will see that sometimes there is nothing you can really do to insure the bird is 100%

safe at all times. Accidents happen all the time. Things like air fresheners, Teflon pans, perfumes, earrings, holiday decorations and many more things than I can mention are always lurking around the corner. Those are things you can prevent the bird from getting injured by for the most part. Then there are things like neighbors who spray pesticides and paint without knowing fumes are toxic and pets like the neighbors cat who spooks the bird and it flies against the back wall of the aviary. What I am saying is that there is no guarantee that the bird is safe at any time. Yes we take a risk when we fly our birds but it is a calculated risk. If we drive a car we might get into an accident, does that mean we stop driving all together? No, we just drive carefully.

A More Detailed Look at Training Flying Recall

Training your bird to come on cue is very important and easier than you think. All you need is a play stand or portable perch, a clicker and your birds favorite treats and you are set to go. This is the biggest step to a successful relationship with a "fully-flighted" parrot and today you will learn just how simple this beginning behavior is to train...

Treats - Motivating Polly
We discuss this in more detail throughout the book but the first step is to find a treat that will motivate your bird to do what you want it to do. When you are first starting you might not know what their favorite treat is so you just offer them a bunch of stuff in your palm or offer it from a bowl and see what they pick first. My Conures always pick Papaya or Pineapple so I train them with that usually, my Macaws usually choose Sunflower Seeds or Peanuts so that's what I usually use for them most of the time. There will be exceptions but Cockatoos normally like Pinenuts best but Safflower Seeds and Star Anise are also favorite treats for many 'toos. My Rosebreasted Cockatoo (also called a Galah) named "Pebbles" Loves Buckwheat, Niger and Hemp seeds. Amazons usually will be pretty motivated for Corn and Sunflower Seeds, I like getting "seed junky" Amazons then switching them to a pellet diet...you have never seen a bird as motivated as an Amazon who is desperate for seeds! Good luck with the Greys, they are picky little guys but you can usually find something they like more than anything like Nutriberries etc. Anyway, once you find a favorite treat you ONLY give it to them for training. This way the bird can eat all day and will still work for the treats you are using. Many trainers starve their birds but I do not recommend this or condone that as a method to motivate a pet bird. Food Management is different than starvation, we are simply controling what kinds of food the bird gets and when. Start with bigger sized treats and gradually get stingy and make them smaller and smaller so eventually they can be eaten faster.

Training The Trick
At first the bird isn't doing any flying at all. All you have to do is turn your palm upwards (this is the cue) as you have the bird step up. When they

step onto your hand click and reward. Repeat this several times having the bird step up on your hand, clicking, then rewarding. There is one piece of advice I can give you here and that is to put the bird back on his/her perch or play stand as it eats the treat, this keeps the bird "stationed" so he isn't chasing you later on when you are walking back and forth requesting the bird to fly longer distances. So have the bird step up, click, reward, then place him on the stand or perch while he eats. After the bird finishes the treat you can start over moving slightly farther away from the bird each time until it is almost falling to reach your hand. From here it is just a waiting game for the bird to take its first flights to you, you will see some definite wing flapping as the bird attempts to reach your hand across the gap that is now forming between you and him. Sometimes you just have to wait the bird out, if they understand the game you will see them thinking about what they have to do. Be patient! One trick to help when you are waiting them out is to then place the treat in your hand to get them to take the first hop. A motivated bird usually can't help but fall for this Lure, and it really seems to make the difference sometimes if they have the treat they desire staring them in the face. Soon they should start hopping to you, then flying to you. Distance does not matter as long as they understand the game. You can increase the distance as far as you feel is necessary and once the bird gets used to flying back to the perch each time to eat his treat it looks very impressive to have a bird flying "laps" back and forth from you to the stand, then back again etc.

Furthering Your Training
You can take this training farther by moving outdoors to an aviary or screened in porch, and after they get used to flying outside you can look around for a decent 2-story apartment complex and take advantage of the stairs and different levels so that the bird gets used to flying up and down instead of just back and forth in a straight line. Have fun and Happy Flying!

Training Flight with Second Hand or Rescue Birds

Some birds are just naturally gifted or more talented than others and it seems like they will dance circles around other birds in half the time with half the training. If you are fortunate enough to have one of these birds you will come to realize that anything is possible! I have one such bird, her name is Cappy (short for Cap'n Crunch) and in my opinion she is the smartest Greenwing Macaw on the planet. She speaks in context, innovates and creates her own behaviors, she can identify several colors and choose whichever you ask her to and sometimes it even seems like she is training me instead of the other way around. Yet the most astounding thing about this bird is the fact that I got her second-hand at 4 years old from a pet store that told me she hated men, was vicious and would attack me etc...

The results I have achieved with her are not typical, and while many will credit her progress with my background as a professional trainer the fact is that she is just one of those birds I described earlier who just exhibits an exceptional aptitude for life as a performance parrot and a very large IQ. There is no denying that some birds will just blow your socks off...but as we discussed earlier in this blog many of the birds you see on TV, DVD's and so on were born into this life and had the desired behaviors shaped from the very beginning by a brilliant trainer who understood the "game" very well. Here I hope to explore the typical way I train birds that come from less than ideal backgrounds. It will be a much longer road than if you were to do it with a baby bird and the baby bird who is trained from infancy to be a show bird is in a whole other "class", yet it is very possible for you to fly your older bird that you have rescued or adopted later in life.

Winning Over A Fearful Bird

For some birds touching or handling them is an advanced behavior. For them it will be necessary to build up a relationship where the bird sees you as a positive entity with whom every interaction means great things will happen. This can take quite some time to manifest but move at the pace of the bird and never rush them. Parrots live a long time so take it slow, there is no reason to rush. When you first bring a bird like this home it may see you as something to fear, something to avoid...and that is what must change. It must cease the attempts to flee and start choosing (and even preferring) to be close to you. One good way to do this is to find it's favorite food and ONLY give it as a treat for training. At first you give the treats freely, such as when you walk by the cage you can simply drop a treat in the bowl and keep walking. Pretty soon the bird will usually start to look forward to seeing you.

Some birds are phobic with hands. They have usually been forced to interact when if they had the choice they would not have. They usually do not have a choice and even after several attempts to flee a situation where they feel threatened many owners persist and continue to expose the bird to this "terrifying" situation. They chase the bird around (usually in an effort to get them to "step up") and there is no escape from this pursuing, predatory animal (the owner) who insists on getting what they want. This is what I mean when I say that many people are unintentionally teaching their birds to hate and bite them. For a bird who is "hand shy" one very good trick is to hold up your hand and at the same time drop a favorite food in the bowl. Start so that you can barely reach the cage to give the treat and as the birds body language shows that it is relaxing you can gradually move closer. What this does is to condition the bird so that it equates the hand it has feared for so long with treats. This can be a slow process but it is worth it! Another trick to accomplish this is to replace the birds food bowl with your hand. On your days off you can just park your butt in front of the cage, put your hand in and fall asleep if you have to. One great way to make this work for you is to take a bird who was used to eating seeds and switch them to pellets...then only offer them seeds from your hand. Give it a week and don't be surprised to have the bird diving onto your hand for it's seeds ;)

Pre-Flight Training
Targeting: The first behavior we will teach the bird is to touch a target on cue. Each time the bird touches the stick it is rewarded with a favorite treat so eventually the bird will run back and forth, up and down ladders

etc in order to reach the target. At this point we introduce the hand. Once the bird will easily step onto your hand to reach the target you want to stop luring him or her and phase out the target...that way you are shaping the actual behavior so that the parrot steps up on cue. While he is still chasing the target give the verbal cue "up" as his foot touches your arm. Immediately click and reward if he continues his chase and touches your arm in the process. From here on you can start to phase out the target by rewarding the foot touching your arm instead of the beak touching the target. After it looks like the bird has got it completely get rid of the target and try just giving the bird his cue. Go back if needed. Now you should be able to hold the arm up, give the cue and he or she steps right up. Now that the bird steps up on cue you continue to work it and work it daily until you say "up" and that foot flies into the air! Make it reflexive - a true "conditioned response" is the goal.

Now that the bird steps up without hesitation you can begin flight training even if the bird is still clipped a little. Not every bird will be willing to take the first flight right away, especially the ones who were clipped before fledging age and never knew to fly. On the other end of the coin, some second hand birds will be very eager flyers and may require a light clip of the first 3 primaries to limit their choices and ability while you shape the behaviors. Each bird is an individual so you will need to decide what is best for your bird...

Training The Recall: To start you will need to decide if you are using just a physical cue (extending your arm and reaching toward the bird or simply turning your palm upwards are the most common) or also pairing it with a verbal cue such as a whistle etc. Simply turning up the hand works well if you are only flying in enclosed spaces but I usually incorporate a whistle eventually if they will ever fly outside. Either way, you will give the cue(s) but at this time you are simply asking the bird to step up. Click and reward the bird, then place it back on it's stand or perch. Do this again and again until eventually you retract your arm a very short distance, each time making sure to place the bird back on his stand after you give it the reward. This distance you move away each time will be barely noticeable to you and the bird so don't move too fast! Making sure they understand the "game" is the most important thing here. Pretty soon most birds (especially birds like Goffins Cockatoos) will be hopping back and forth between your hand when you give the cue and then back to his perch when you reward him. Getting an older bird in the air may be difficult but it can be done if you are patient and they are motivated enough. Move at the pace of the bird. After they are hopping or taking small flights using 1-2 flaps you can start moving farther and farther away until they are flying longer distances back and forth between you and the stand. Many birds get pretty creative when they get to this point and may not only fly directly back and forth in a straight line...it will almost always fly from point A to point B but kit may zig-zag or fly a circle or add extra "steps" you didn't specifically train it to do. I love this stuff because crowds really seem to like it and it is a demonstration in the parrots' creativity and intelligence, it shows the flaws of operant conditioning, and you get to see more of the natural flight patterns these birds were born to do.

Advanced Flight Training

Earlier we took a look at the mother of all behaviors that we train birds to do: Teaching them to fly. When we consider the amount of evolution and adaptation that occurred over millions of years to get birds in the air it could almost be considered amusing that we trainers put so much thought, time and energy on something so very natural. Birds have evolved air sacs in the place of lungs which makes them more suited for flight, they have evolved hollow skeletal structures to lighten the load, their wrists are turned backwards from the way many other animals are designed and the most obvious adaptation of course is the body being covered in feathers. Flying is what they do, but having an intelligent creature like a parrot and giving it the ability to choose whether or not it wants to fly to you or take off into the vast horizon can be very intimidating to most people. This is the topic of today's article: flighted parrots and allowing them choice.

In the last flight training article we discussed my process of raising a baby show bird from infancy and shaping the behavior of flight from the very beginning. I also taught you how you could train older birds to do this using Targeting. While an older bird can and will perform excellently most of the time I DO NOT believe older birds are equipped with the same "toolbox" that my handfed babies are and it may not always be in their best interest to allow them free-flight outdoors. If you do not have the option to finish hand feeding a baby for use in flight training I suggest you get one as close to weaning age as possible, even then the difference between a couple of weeks is such a big difference that I strongly caution you to decide what is in the birds best interest before deciding to continue to advanced flight training. If your bird does the things we looked at in the last article then you should be very proud because that is already more than the majority of bird owners have done. Many adult birds can only realistically be expected to fly indoors and if you wish to bring the lessons outside you do so at your own risk. It would be much safer to work on the lessons in the last article, gain some experience, and then acquire an infant and start over with a new bird before you graduate to the great outdoors.

In the last article we built the foundations for a super parrot. Basically what we did was taught the bird to recall (come to you on cue) and in much simpler terms we trained it to fly in a "relay", also known as "point to point" where the bird flies from Point A to Point B. We also discussed shaping the "Turn Around" so that the bird would fly in circles (which basically has the bird flying from Point A back to Point A again). Through Targeting you learned you could teach the bird to fly from Point A to Point B to Point C and land anywhere else you desired them to, because as we know: wherever the beak goes the body follows. You could spend a lifetime training birds to do this and be considered a very successful trainer but there is still so much more out there to train!

Today we will look at the styles of flying where the bird has more choices and is essentially left to his or her own devices for a period of time. This form of flight training is a big reason why I DO NOT use weight management to train the majority of parrots; because anybody who has practiced Falconry knows a fully flighted bird who is too hungry or too full can become unresponsive and start doing their own thing. To train a parrot to do this you can use favorite treats to reinforce the behaviors you seek, but you must also rely increasingly on other forms of reinforcement such as social interests and play interests (These are "secondary reinforcers" which we discussed earlier).

I would like to point out for clarification purposes that even though I started working with birds of prey at a very young age, the first birds I ever worked with and the first birds I ever flew were parrots, so my training style is NOT falconry based as many other trainers who hear of my background have been so quick to say. This is a form of training that is specifically adapted to parrots, who have adapted much differently than birds of prey. That is not to say that Falconry techniques have no value, on the other hand I feel it is quite the opposite and that other forms of training translate very well from species to species. I have used the positive reinforcement techniques that I use on parrots to train raptors and had them flying without jesses or any other forms of restraints. This does not mean that I feel Falconry techniques have no value, again that is not my view it is just an opinion many other trainers who are flying parrots these days. Falconry has many lessons for any trainer, such as the widely held belief that an intermittent reward is a stronger reinforcer than simply rewarding the bird each time he or she does something correctly.

So we have already studied Relay/Point to Point flying, now we will explore another form of flying where the bird is flown without as much guidance or "rules" and the bird can fly wherever it wants to fly. Some trainers call this Free Style, some call it "at liberty flying" and others make a distinction between the two and view both Free Style and "at liberty flying" as different entities all together. To me they are essentially the same but whenever someone talks about "at liberty flying" it generally means the bird has more choices when it comes to several things such as where it will land, when it will return to the handler and how long it will remain in the air. As I said, to me these are just varying degrees of the same thing and the separation just complicates the issue of training flight behaviors for new or perspective trainers.

The point I must make to you is that even though you will be allowing the bird to come back whenever it chooses to you MUST only attempt this with a bird that has a strong Recall response and will come back to you on cue if needed. In order to allow the bird totally unstructured free-flight this must be taken into consideration for safety's sake. Now the reason a baby bird makes such a good candidate for this training is because in the wild they are hardwired to stay close to the parents for quite some time after they leave the nest, this is instinctive and can be thought of like a natural harness that mother nature gave us. But we can only use this harness if we raised the bird. Once you have the bird performing everything we talked about in the blog article "Flight Training Secrets Revealed" you would take it outside and instead of cueing it to come back to you just start walking away. The bird will see this and 9 times out of 10 they will immediately try to follow you, reward the bird with his favorite treat and practice this a few more times. Place him in a small tree or other object and work on the recall 2 or 3 times, then place him in the tree and again just start walking away. This will start to get the bird used to thinking on his own and making its own choices.

I have also trained macaws to do this in Las Vegas over a few different golf courses and it was simple. The client wanted to be able to take the birds anywhere and free-fly them so I trained them to return to a trailer for positive reinforcement (food). I would stand inside the trailer, cue the bird and when he flew inside he got his dinner. I gradually increased the distance over time until the bird was flying quite some distance to get to his dinner. This was just A to B flying. Then we placed the birds in front of the trailer and I didn't even have to cue them, they had become so conditioned to eating only from the perch in the trailer that they did it on their own and could be allowed true free-flight from then on because they had been trained to enter the trailer at will. We also began to hide treats around in different trees in an effort to stimulate the birds' natural foraging instincts and get them to start investigating their environment. This got them flying from tree to tree to different perches etc. These are now birds who rely on their own decision making and decide when they will return, hence the term "at liberty".

Besides training this for a few entertainers I have also done this with a flock of 200 cockatiels at a breeding facility in Nevada. These were not tame and socialized birds but were wild, parent raised birds that had babies in the nest in some cases. At first I conditioned them to eat only from a specific red dish inside the flight. After they got used to this I would stand in the flight and hold the dish so they became more accustomed to me. After only about a month I had all 200 birds flying to me inside the cage using no cues or other signals (visual or audible) to make this happen. Afterwards we increased the distance so that they were flying outside of the enclosures doors to land on the red dish. Again this was Point to Point or A to B flying at first but now we had them actually exiting the flight in order to reach to red dish. Afterwards I started just leaving the doors open and allowing them to do their own thing for longer periods until I "called" them with the red food dish. Now the owner leaves the doors open year round and the flight cage is only used as a roost where the birds spend the night and raise their young. I have heard other trainers say not to fly cockatiels due to their being r-type animals who rely more on over-breeding to survive instead of k-type animals who usually produce fewer offspring but have a higher intelligence and the parents invest more time into them (most parrots and highly intelligent animals are k-type) but this has NO bearing on trainability or capacity for flight training and many smaller birds like Budgies and Cockatiels can actually learn a wide variety of behaviors including flight.

The purpose of this article and my previous article on flight (Flight Training Secrets Revealed) is to demystify this form of training and to make some sane techniques available to a wider variety of trainers who wish to explore this amazing behavior. There is a wealth of misinformation available on the internet and it seems that if you are on a training website these days it is either complete garbage or a get rich quick scheme (or both in some cases). The truth is this form of training really isn't as complicated as the people performing in shows or charging you for a seminar want you to believe. These are techniques I use every day to train birds for television, Las Vegas shows, entertainers, educational birds and much more and I have seen there is a hunger for this information in the bird world...but unfortunately the demand is much greater than the supply. Feel free to share this and any of my articles with any bird lover you know - happy flying!

A Closer Look at Diet

These days everywhere you look you are being told to feed your birds pellets. Seed diets have recently gone from being accepted for parrot consumption to being demonized and regarded as "bad bird keeping". My mom was keeping birds over 35 years ago. At that time commercialized diets for pet birds were almost nonexistent and she was mixing her own blends of species specific food to feed her many wild-caught parrots, which ranged from little Cherry Headed Conures to a large and loud Mollucan Cockatoo. Within my lifetime spent living with birds I have seen many changes in the way we care for them, but today we will discuss my professional opinion regarding the ideal parrot diet – after all, you are what you eat...

Pelleted diets are the "go to" diets to feed these days, it seems like everyone is jumping on the band wagon including Veterinarians who many people regard as being the all knowing God-like figures who we trust with the lives of our birds. Many times we take our bird for a wellness exam directly after purchasing them from a pet store, breeder or rescue if you are lucky enough to have a rescue that adopts birds out in your area. From that very first visit the "pellet push" starts and before you know it you are paying for the most expensive parrot food in existence. Now, paying large amounts of money for bird food would be something I would completely support if it was truly the healthiest option for our birds - but it is not!

The selling point for many purchasers is the fact that seeds are supposedly "unhealthy" for our birds, but take a closer look at the number 1 ingredient in Harrisons Pelleted Diets and you will see Flax Seed! Harrisons is distributed by most veterinarians who accept avian patients but make no mistake - the vets that distribute these pellets are paid to do so. So we are told that seeds are bad so we must feed pellets but they too are made of seeds? How confusing...

But not all pellets are made of seeds, Roudybush is peanut-based which spoils quicker than any other brand, gets "buggy" in the summer and may contain deadly Mycotoxins if the oil from the peanuts becomes rancid. Other pellets are wheat-based which can cause severe allergic reactions in many birds and if they are not the "natural" variety often contain harmful dyes and fragrances. How harmful are these added dyes you ask? Well, the red dye commonly used for pelleted diets has been marked as unsafe for human consumption by the FDA, so why is it acceptable to feed it to our birds? There is also the fact that pellets are supposed to be a "complete" diet and many times you are not supposed to add ANY extras to the diet. Why? Because when a bird has an overdose of certain vitamins it can be deadly, and if you feed certain foods or supplements in conjunction with some kinds of pellets this can certainly cause Hypervitaminosis. This causes countless ailments in our birds ranging from curled toenails to overgrown beaks to acute liver failure.

Besides all of this there is one reason which stands out to me as being the biggest point I can make that will hopefully persuade you NOT to feed a pellet only diet: Environmental Stimulation, or the lack of. Parrots come from places of such abundance; many species such as Psittacula Parakeets have been documented eating different foods every single day. As the seasons change so does the menu, and even if the seasons didn't change there is such a diversity of plant life in the habitats of many birds that they still wouldn't eat the same food every single day of the year. I am of the opinion that pellets do not provide enough stimulation for our birds that spend most of the day locked in the cage while we go out to earn a living. With that having been said, I do include many different brands of pellets into my parrots daily feeding regimen, but it is a tiny amount usually only about a teaspoon or 10% of the diet. Anybody who has ever visited these animals in the wild knows for a fact that there aren't many bowls of pellets laying around or growing in the tree tops. So what do I feed? Read on to find out...

Quinoa - The Super Grain
This is a South American grain commonly found in health food stores. Its nutritional benefits exceed many other grains, especially the protein content which is nearly double that of most others. It contains Calcium,

Phosphorous, Vitamins E & B and Potassium. You can sprout it or mix 2 parts water to 1 part quinoa and cook it for 10 minutes and your birds will love it! I add vegetables, berries or anything else I have lying around or sometimes I just feed it plain. One trick is to add a cinnamon stick when you cook it and it absorbs the flavor into the quinoa, I have never met a bird who could resist this for long! There are also plenty of products available that contain quinoa such as bread, pasta and cereal.

Wheat Grass - The Amazing Holistic Plant
Wheat grass is also common in health food stores and with all the health benefits this wonderful little plant can provide it is not surprising that it has recently grown in popularity. You can grow it yourself or you can buy it from farmers markets if you don't have a local health food supply store in your area. This amazing grass contains Chlorophyll which protects from carcinogens and helps to remove pollutants from the bloodstream. It detoxifies the bloodstream by increasing the amount of oxygen and it also repairs and helps to cleans the liver. Wheat grass also contains Choline, Potassium & Magnesium which is also very beneficial to the liver. There is as much Vitamin A as carrots. In addition to these, Liquid Oxygen is also present in wheat grass which improves circulation due to expansion of the blood vessels. Folic Acid, Calcium, Vitamins C, E, B12, and Iron are also included in every blade of wheat grass. Wheat grass has also been shown to improve and/or restore fertility and UC San Diego did a study using different types of grasses and found that it is possible to repair damaged DNA with compounds naturally occurring in wheat grass.

Sprouted Seeds, Grains and Legumes
In the wild a parrot's diet consists mainly of living food. It is very healthy to recreate this diet for our birds and it has never been easier. The easiest to start with will be Mung Beans, these are very healthy and you shouldn't have any problems getting these to sprout. Safflower Seeds are amazingly healthy for your bird no matter what any "anti seed" skeptics say. Doctors recommend drinking safflower oil for our own heart health so why not include this in your parrot's diet as well? Sunflower Seeds, Alfalfa and Lentils are also great for sprouting and your birds will love them. Any

breeder who is not feeding their birds sprouts will be amazed at the increase in production rates and rescue birds or any others who are presenting FDB's (feather destructive behaviors) will benefit as well. I also sprout feed designed for Racing Pigeons and feed it to my parrots. Soak Mix, Soak & Cook or Soak & Simmer products are also great for our birds. Even if seeds have a bad reputation they are high in Vitamins A,B,D & E, Calcium, Phosphorus and they contain Unsaturated Fatty Oils that are an essential component to having healthy feathers, beaks and skin. Tell that to the next person who calls seeds "junk food" or says you are feeding your birds candy every time they hear you feed some seeds.

Aloe - The Unknown Super Food
Many people don't know it but Aloe Vera is a nutritionally complete food and the FDA has evaluated and approved it as a food substance. Out of over 150,000 botanical specimens this has the highest content of nutrients essential to our existence. It contains substantial amounts of over 39 essential minerals and vitamins and all of the Amino Acids. A lack of Amino Acids in our birds can cause allergies and if you know of any birds suffering from skin or plumage ailments like feather plucking be sure to give them access to this. Aloe is also great for birds suffering from digestive or intestinal disorders. It also greatly boosts the Immune System, guarding our birds from infectious disease, allergies etc. This is also something I recommend feeding to birds who have been diagnosed with or are suspected of having Fatty Liver Disease. You can offer it to them as fresh stalks, cut into thin slices or you can add the drinking gel found at most health stores directly to their water.

Sweet Potatoes
Relatively unheard of as a food for birds this is a seriously underestimated addition to a healthy parrots diet and many bird keepers who try this end up feeding it to their birds on a daily basis. These are very high in Fiber and Complex Carbohydrates and low in calories. They also contain Vitamins C, B-6 and Potassium. One half cup contains 23,000 IU's of Beta Carotene which is a powerful antioxidant known to prevent Cancer and Heart Disease. This can be offered several different ways but I usually boil

it and offer it to the birds as part of the mix of sprouts and other soft foods. This can also be mashed for younger parrots and makes an excellent weaning food.

Eggs - Incredible, Edible and Great For Our Birds
t 93.7%, eggs score higher than any other food when it comes to Protein content. They contain all 9 essential Amino Acids and are a great way to sneak some extra Calcium into the diet if you include some of the shell. I usually offer them hard boiled but many birds seem to like them better scrambled. If you make Birdie Bread you can also add some shell to this and it will be especially beneficial to egg-laying hens.

Conclusion
My advice to you is to take all of these ingredients and combine them together as a staple diet for your pet birds. You can add seasonally available items to this as you wish. I take the small amount of pellets that I feed and other things such as Birdie Bread and I place them in different areas of the cage or flight which creates an interesting and stimulating environment when you also have toys, swings, various perches etc. We should always stimulate the foraging instincts of our birds whenever possible because being a "perch potato" just isn't healthy. One great invention are the "bird kabobs" that you skewer different fruits and vegetables on and place around the cage. These things will definitely keep Polly busy while you are at work all day. Other great additions to the diet are Apples, Tofu, Flowers, Nuts, Broccoli, Brussel Sprouts, Cabbage, Cauli Flower, Chard, Kale, Mustard Greens, Carrots, Corn, Turnips, Papaya and Blueberries. Strawberries are great as well, but be sure that they are organic because strawberries have the highest pesticide content of any other produce and since they grow on the ground there are also plenty of fungicides as well.

Food Management

In a society where instant gratification runs rampant, many people want "McTraining" methods that resemble a fast food establishment. The majority of DVD's, online experts and chat room parrot gurus feed this craving with one-size-fits-all approaches to parrot problem solving. The truth is, some birds have had a very hard life and for them stepping up or being handled is more of an "advanced" behavior to train. Today I will share what has worked for me. This is called Food Management and is a great starting point for novice trainers.

The first thing we need to ask ourselves is what kind of relationship do we have with the bird already? When we walk in the room, does the bird exhibit fearful body language? Does he run to the back of the cage and hide?

If the bird sees you as something to escape or avoid that is the first thing that needs to change. When we walk in the room we want that bird to be eager to work with us, so this is where we would begin to manage the animals' diet in a more productive way that will allow us to gain his or her trust. Make no mistake, not all parrots have to be trained using food rewards – some will work for "secondary reinforcers" such as praise, affection, a favorite toy and so forth but these birds are not what we are here to discuss today. The birds we are talking about are the "rescues".

To manage the animals' food we need to first observe him/her to see what their favorite food items are. Give them a large bowl filled with plenty of variety in food choices and see what they pick 1st, 2nd, 3rd and so on. Do this over a few days offering different foods each time and soon you will have a very good idea of what foods your bird loves and which foods it seems indifferent to.

Now that we know what the birds favorite foods are we ONLY feed them those foods as rewards during training sessions when they have performed correctly or taken a step towards your goal. Now, for many people this raises an emotional issue because they feel like they are withholding food from their birds and they feel it is "wrong" to deny him or her treats or make their bird "work" for food. The truth is, all we are doing is MANAGING the food, we are NOT withholding it. Think about it like this: If we feed the parrot one bowl of food every day the only food he has is in that bowl. If his favorite food is peanuts, he can only eat as many as you put in his food dish. So everyday he gets 2 or 3 peanuts. But if he is working to earn those peanuts as a reward during training sessions he can have AS MANY AS HE WANTS! He could have 10 of them if he performs well, so are we really withholding food if he was only receiving 3 a day? The birds I work with where I have managed their food typically get much more of that favorite food than they used to get when they were free fed.

The easiest birds to train have all been seed-junkies: Take a 30 year old parrot that has been fed sunflower seeds his entire life and convert him to an all pellet diet supplemented with seeds as training rewards - you have never seen such a motivated bird!

The best way to have success with food management is to set up a training diet. Many birds will eat about 20% of their weight in food each day. Parrots typically eat 2 times per day in the wild, so this can be mimicked in the home by feeding the bird 2 meals daily instead of one large meal. We would then schedule training sessions around those meals so that we have the biggest impact on our birds because they are more motivated for food if they are trained on an empty stomach. I typically feed a "salad" in the morning made of vegetables, fruits, sprouts and so on and in the evening they get pellets. Before we feed those meals we would train the bird – so if you are feeding the salad at 8am and the pellets for dinner at 6pm we would train at 7:00-7:30am and also at 5:00-5:30pm daily.

*NOTE After about an hour you should remove the food to prevent spoilage and also to keep the bird on schedule. Leaving the food in the bird's cage or enclosure is the most common mistake I see beginning trainers make. If you leave the bowls until the next session/feeding you will not have very productive training sessions.

So, to recap what we are doing here is motivating the bird a couple different ways: The first thing we are doing is making his 1 daily feeding into 2 smaller feedings. The next thing we are doing is taking the food he sees as the most "valuable" and giving it even more value because it is harder to come by.

We should start to see an impact in the bird's behavior right away because we are making him want to do what we want him to do. What we are trying to accomplish is getting the bird to do things we want by choice. These things could be entering the cage or carrier willingly, stepping up, interacting politely with different handlers or multiple family members and so on. We are finding the most positive, least intrusive solution. I hope you give Food Management a chance; I'd love to hear how it has helped your bird and your relationship with him.

Weight Management Training Demystified

Weight Management (WM) and Food Management (FM) are used by animal trainers every day; however, this is something many experienced trainers only understand the basics of. This means that when newer or lesser-experienced trainers set out to train an animal using these techniques they often do not fully understand what they are doing right or wrong, why it is or is not working for them, and how to improve their training skills altogether. I train many birds for free flight each year and often times when training an older bird, wild caught, or parent reared bird, I will utilize WM, because the animal with a challenging background normally sees you as something to avoid in the beginning and this helps to change that and allows you to build a trainer/student relationship, as well as properly motivating the animal to respond to your cues and actively seek direction as a way to earn rewards. Both techniques are using Primary Reinforcement so I will not discuss Secondary Reinforcers here.

Simply put, the most common form of Food Management (FM) is either 1: making it so that the bird ONLY eats during training (popular with early Behaviorists such as B.F. Skinner while he trained animals in a laboratory setting, they would become conditioned to perform a certain behavior such as pushing a lever which would earn them a reward - this was NOT normally requested of the animal by the trainer or done on cue), or 2: you discover the animals' favorite food items and only offer those during training - meanwhile the bird is given less desirable food items that it can eat at its leisure. A good example where #2 is useful is when we begin training a bird who was previously fed an all-seed diet, we would convert the bird to pellets which it would view as less desirable than the seeds and therefore it would then value the seeds as a reward during training. The animal would ONLY get the seeds during training sessions. They can still have all the pellets they want and can eat all day, but when done properly they are still sufficiently motivated to earn the seeds even with a visibly full crop in some cases.

Weight Management (WM) on the other hand is FM taken a step further; the trainer carefully maintains the animals' weight within a certain range, often called a "target weight", "working weight", "fly weight" or "flying weight". It is hard for novice trainers to imagine working with a freshly caught bird of prey for example, but professionals deal with these birds all the time. The animal might have been flying wild only a very short time ago and often has a natural fear of humans. Weight Management is crucial to those practicing Falconry or working with performing birds that will perform high-profile behaviors where the bird is given lots of choices as to whether or not they will continually behave the way we desire them to. If you are giving a presentation and the bird flies off, the entertainer or trainer giving the presentation can call the bird back at will if the animal is trained properly. They willingly return because doing so earns them a food reward. The goal of a trainer who uses WM should always be to fly or work the bird at the highest weight possible while still maintaining good responses from the bird. A bird flown at too high a weight may become unresponsive. They can start doing their own thing and ignoring the cues we give them which is bad for all involved.

There are many opportunities to make mistakes and the most common is to underfeed or overfeed the bird. Disaster can occur either way so attention to detail is key. Smaller birds especially will need to be weighed as much as 3 times per day in some cases to accurately gauge and control the weight within a certain parameter. Sometimes maintenance within a 10th of a gram is required for smaller species, so it can be very intimidating. Do not make the mistake of thinking the fly weight will be the same with every member of a species, for example, many people see me flying a bird and wish to do the same with their pet back home and I get asked questions such as "What is the flying weight for a Galah"? The answer is that it will be different with each bird and even changes from time to time with an individual animal as we "fine tune" them to perform the best they can (which is a constant process). A bird flying at 86 grams at one point in time might be flying at 78 grams later on and again at around 93 grams only a few months later. Fly weights should never be static. Again we should always be working towards flying or working at the highest weight possible. Once we find out a good working weight we ever so slightly begin to raise them up until eventually they can be flying well above the weight they would be at even if they were allowed unlimited access to food all day every day.

Before we begin training a bird using WM we first have to record their "ad lib" weight, which is the weight of the bird if it was on "free-feed" or "feed-up" (free-feed is allowing the bird unlimited access to food and feed-up is when we allow the bird to eat as much as it wants a few times per day but we remove the bowls to prevent spoilage etc in between feedings.) Measure the weight of the food the bird is eating each day so you know exactly how much he is eating to maintain the ad lib weight. Once we determine the ad lib weight and the amount of food required to sustain that weight we can begin training using WM.

When we first begin the bird will typically shy away or bate or even nearly injure itself trying to avoid you in some cases. This is normal when working with wild-caught birds, fearful birds, rescues and so on. At first they might not even take a treat from your hand when you offer one freely but this is normal when working with challenging subjects and you shouldn't let this discourage you. As the days progress the animals' natural motivation for food sets in and this becomes a thing of the past as they come to see you as pleasant (a food source) instead of something they need to fear or avoid. It is amazing to have a bird take its first hops to your arm when they were viciously attacking you only a week before.

The following is a demonstration of Weight Management with a Greenwinged Macaw

Say the ad lib weight was 1000 grams when you first start. The bird is fed equal portions of seeds, pellets and vegetables, yet when given a choice he prefers the seeds and eats them first – so these will be reserved for training only and he can have the pellets and fruits/vegetables left in the cage or aviary to eat at will. The bird tries to avoid you as soon as you walk in the room and it won't even take a food treat from you even though it has not been fed yet this morning. You immediately drop a treat in the bowl and leave the room which ends the session on the best note possible. The birds' weight is dropped 15 grams by reducing the amount of food given (pellets and vegetables are reduced, the seeds remain the same amount) leaving his new target weight at 985 grams. That might seem excessive but bear with me; the drop in weight is only just over 1% (and usually the bird is a bit overweight before training begins). After trying this weight again next day it is slightly more responsive but only for a moment so the weight is lowered again by another 15 grams to a target weight of 970 grams that the bird will work at the following day. That is exactly 3% reduction in weight from the original ad lib weight where the bird was allowed to eat as much as it wants but the results are already very noticeable the next day. You are able to begin training the flying recall indoors for a short time before it becomes full. Since the bird only remained responsive for a short time we again decrease the weight by 10 grams leaving his new target weight at 960 grams. Now the bird is performing reliably for short sessions flying Point A to Point B Recalls on cue (flies to you when asked) indoors for a few days and he really seems like a new bird. The animal has transformed from fearful or aggressive bird into a bird that reliably performs a behavior on cue. We have achieved this by simply reducing an already overweight birds' body mass by only 4%.

We maintain him at this weight until eventually the bird is introduced to a new handler. Upon introduction of the new person the bird becomes unresponsive and we observe a breakdown in his behavior. We again reduce the weight, this time by 10 grams leaving his new fly weight at 950 grams. He does poorly over the next few days so we once again reduce the weight by 10 grams leaving him at 6% less weight than free-feed and weighing 940 grams. He improves remarkably and even when we move outdoors without restraints he is reliable. We teach him to fly from A to B on cue, Station on a platform above the stage, fly from trainer to trainer and he is right on target learning quickly and becoming increasingly confident when exposed to new and different objects and situations.

Here is where the more experienced trainer will begin slowly increasing the birds' weight, while the new or inexperienced trainer keeps the bird at his target weight of 940. If you paid attention you will notice we dropped the bird's weight in chunks of 10-15 grams each time – but now that we are raising it back again we do this very slowly and meticulously because we increase the body weight at a much slower rate than when we decrease the weight. You do not want the increase in food/weight to be noticeable to the animal. So we only raise the bird 1-5 grams a day. We have him working well until we get all the way back up to 985 grams, when we begin to train a new behavior and the bird needs a bit more motivation. We reduce him to 975 grams and the problem is fixed – but the lesser experienced trainer is still working the bird at 940, so he drops the weight to 925 grams while my bird is performing the same quality at 970 grams . That is a difference of 45 grams and we have only just begun. Now we introduce the bird to crowds, cameras, lights and so forth. I had increased his weight over time to 1005 grams and he was working fine until now. I reduce his weight to 995 and the problem is fixed for my bird – but the other trainers bird is still at 925 and is still reduced further to 915. Now we are at a difference of 80 grams between my bird and the other trainers' bird. I slowly increase the weight over time all the way until the bird is flying at 1025 when he finally gets unresponsive and/or responding too slow to my cues so I cut him back 10 grams and he is performing superbly at 1015 – 100 grams heavier than the bird trained the old fashioned way and 15 grams ABOVE the ad lib weight that he would be at if he were just left in a cage eating all day. How is this possible?

The secret is that there is a "mental hunger" that can be used. The birds' weight is reduced in quick, noticeable increments but when we increase the weight it is not noticeable, so even though the bird weighs 1015, he is still mentally working and flying at 940 grams. This psychological hunger was first used by trainer Steve Martin to my knowledge and is very important to use because having the animal at higher weight means the bird is healthier, less prone to disease and infection etc. I can't stress enough that we want the bird flying at the highest weight possible. Flying at the highest weight possible is the most positive, least intrusive solution and that should be the goal of all animal trainers across the globe, regardless of the species of animals you are working with. From raptors to penguins to parrots, all of these will respond to this technique. It was my hope in writing this that the people wishing to train birds using WM would have a decent starting point explained by a professional member of IAATE (International Association of Avian Trainers and Educators) and for those of you who are already utilizing weight management I hope that the idea of psychological hunger finds its' way into your "toolbox". Food Management, Weight Management, even food rewards themselves are not the end of the road for the avian trainer. Always strive to explore new territories and grow.

About The Author

Chris Harris is an avian trainer and consultant currently living in Los Angeles California. He has provided Training, Consultations, Performing Parrots, or other services to The Western Veterinary Conference, Relativity Media, HBO Television Network, Serenity Park Bird Sanctuary, Association for Parrot C.A.R.E., Lockwood Animal Rescue Center, Leftfield Productions, Cirque Du Soleil, The History Channel, Clark County Animal Control, Lied Animal Shelter/The Animal Foundation (Las Vegas, NV), Boones Animals for Hollywood, The Superstars of Magic Show, The Sahara Hotel & Casino in Las Vegas, The National Geographic Channel, Gilcrease Nature Sanctuary, Reptacular Animals, Parrot Mountain, Demand Media (DM), and many other amazing people, companies and projects.

Made in the USA
Lexington, KY
01 May 2015